77,000 Churches

77,000
CHURCHES

PORTER ROUTH

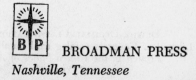

BROADMAN PRESS
Nashville, Tennessee

© 1964 · BROADMAN PRESS
Nashville, Tennessee

422–213

DEWEY DECIMAL CLASSIFICATION: 286
Library of Congress catalog card number: 64–15099
Printed in the United States of America
12.JY64KSP

Contents

Dedicated to My Wife
RUTH
Who Encouraged Me in This Study

Preface

This volume grows out of a conviction that the test of any movement or celebration such as the Baptist Jubilee Advance is to be found in the quality of committed life reflected in the life of the churches. Preaching and teaching have a part in the development of that life. Missions has been an expression or token of the depth of compassion.

Seven Baptist bodies have been involved in the Baptist Jubilee Advance. Unfortunately, lines of communication were little used for many years. There are areas of difference and a variety of methods, but there are large areas of agreement in basic theology. There are extremes in all Baptist groups who clamor for attention, but the wide, silent road of common faith runs through all of the groups without much turning.

The historical review and the brief sketch of organization for the various groups are intended only to be introductory. The selections of sermons, addresses, essays, or personalities are not intended to represent major points of view or thinking in the respected groups. No selections were used from preachers or authors who are still living.

The sketches of the ministers, teachers, and laymen present more Southern Baptists than others only because of the press of time and the expected readership of this volume.

PORTER ROUTH

1
A Story of Beginnings

On a cold February 19, 1812, the sailing schooner *Caravan* slipped from its wharf at Salem, Massachusetts, and made its way toward the gray, open sea and its final destination of Calcutta, India, with Adoniram Judson and Ann Hasseltine Judson aboard. A week later another sailing schooner, the *Harmony*, sailed from Philadelphia with Luther Rice aboard. The two were to meet again in August in Calcutta and to start a chain of events which was to lead to the organization of the General Missionary Convention of the Baptist Denomination in the United States of America for Foreign Missions on May 18, 1814.

One hundred and fifty years later, the 2,500 churches and 150,000 members of 1814 had grown to more than 77,000 churches with a combined membership of more than 20,000,-000 baptized converts. This number represents about 5,000,-000 nonresident members and many churches lacking a vision of world service. The membership figures do not include nearly 5,000,000 children who are touched by the churches in some way but do not count as baptized members. The membership figures do not include some 2,000,000 Baptists in perhaps 3,000 churches who are related to the General Association of Regular Baptists, the Conservative Baptists, the Fellowship of Evangelical Baptist Churches in Canada, the Baptist Bible Fellowship, the American Baptist Association, and other smaller Baptist groups.

The pioneer missionary work of William Carey in India was largely responsible for the commitment and witness of Judson and Rice. William Carey, an English Baptist, is credited with being the leader of the modern missionary movement. He was born of middle-class parents at Paulersbury, England, August 17, 1761, and died June 9, 1834, in Serampore, India. The modern missionary movement gained a new sense of direction and urgency during this seventy-five-year period.

As most English boys of that time, William Carey grew up in the established Anglican Church. He tells us of his conversion to Christ and transfer to the Dissenters in his diary:

February 10, 1779, which being appointed a day of fasting and prayer, I attended worship on that day. Mr. Chater (Congregationalist) of Olney preached, but from what text I have forgotten. He insisted much on following Christ entirely, and enforced his exhortation with that passage, "Let us therefore go out unto him without the camp, bearing his reproach."—Hebrews 13.13. I think I had a desire to follow Christ; but one idea occurred to my mind on hearing those words which broke me off from the Church of England. The idea was certainly very crude, but useful in bringing me from a lifeless, carnal ministry to one more evangelical. I concluded that the Church of England, as established by law, was the camp in which all were protected from the scandal of the cross, and that I ought to bear the reproach of Christ among the dissenters; and accordingly I always afterward attended divine worship among them.

The extreme Calvinism of the Dissenters introduced Carey to a rigid fatalism, which he also rejected, and finally he met with a group of Baptists who seemed to express, in their allegiance to the Word of God and their dedication to liberty, something of the beating of his own heart.

On the twentieth anniversary of the Baptist Missionary Society in England, Dr. John Ryland, pastor of Bristol, recalled: "On October 5, 1783, I baptized in the Néne, just beyond Doddridge's meeting-house, a poor journeyman-shoemaker, little thinking that before nine years elapsed he would prove the first instrument of forming a Society for sending missionaries from England to the heathen world, and much less that he later would become professor of languages in an Oriental college, and a translator of the Scriptures into eleven different tongues."

The ground was being prepared for a new missionary thrust. The ministers of Scotland, inspired by the preaching of George Whitefield, had sent out a memorial in 1744 inviting other Christian groups to pray "that God's Kingdom may come." In America Jonathan Edwards had issued a call for prayer in a powerful sermon.

At a meeting of the Nottinghamshire Baptist Association in 1791, after a sermon by Andrew Fuller exhorting the Baptists to greater zeal, William Carey introduced the question of making some attempt to send the gospel to the heathen. There was not much interest stimulated and one account (not authenticated) recorded that Carey was told God would save the heathen if he wanted to in his own way. The association did request that Carey publish a manuscript he had prepared on "An Enquiry into the Obligations of Christians to Use Means for the Conversion of the Heathen," which has become one of the historic documents of the missionary movement. At the meeting of the annual association in May of 1792, Carey was called on to preach the annual sermon and he used as his text Isaiah 54:2-3 in delivering his historic sermon on "Expect Great Things from God, Attempt Great Things for God."

One biographer said of the sermon, "It was as if the sluices of his soul were thrown fully open, and the flood that had been accumulating for years rushed forth in full force and irresistible power." Despite Carey's seriousness and sense of dedication, no action was proposed by the association, and it was only after an earnest personal appeal to Andrew Fuller during the lunch hour that a decision was made in the meeting "that a plan be prepared against the next ministers' meeting at Kettering for the establishment of a society for the propagation of the gospel among the heathen."

The next meeting of the Nottinghamshire Association was on October 2, 1792. After the public meeting was held, twelve relatively obscure men met in the home of a widow, Mrs. Beedy Wallis, and with a little show of enthusiasm they organized the first British society for the evangelization of the heathen. Members of the society made an offering of nearly sixty dollars, but, more important, William Carey declared his own willingness to go to any part of the world the society might decide to send him.

Word of missionary concern in England crossed the Atlantic. Carey wrote from India to the Massachusetts Missionary Society which had been organized in 1803. William Staughton, who was present as a young man at the meeting in Kettering, became a pastor in the young United States. Under the leadership of Samuel J. Mills, four students at Williams College were having a prayer meeting on a hot August day in 1804 when a rain drove them to a haystack. Out of that first haystack prayer meeting held by the students of Williams College, there came the organization of the "society of inquiry on the subject of missions." Among the students in this group who later dedicated their lives in missionary service was Luther Rice.

Luther Rice was born into the home of a sea captain in Northborough, Massachusetts, on March 25, 1783, the ninth in a family of ten children. His family were members of the Congregational church but were not too zealous in its service.

A few years later, Adoniram Judson was born in Malden, Massachusetts, on August 9, 1788. His father was a pastor of the First Congregational Church in Malden at the time.

In 1809 young Judson entered the Andover Theological Seminary and there he met with Samuel Newell, Samuel Nott,

James Richards, Samuel J. Mills, and Gordon Hall—all had been members of the society at Williams College. Luther Rice arrived at Andover in 1810 and the band of missionary volunteers known as "the Brethren" reached seven members. These students presented a petition to the Congregationalist associational meeting in Bradford, and so earnest were they that it led to the organization of the American Board of Commissioners for Foreign Missions. A historic ordination service took place in the Tabernacle Church in Salem, Massachusetts, on February 6, 1812. Among those appointed were Luther Rice and Adoniram Judson, who had recently married Ann Hasseltine. Luther Rice was also engaged to be married, but the young lady broke the engagement because of his missionary purpose.

One of the historic missionary messages of this early day was delivered by Dr. Leonard Woods, professor at Andover Seminary. Dr. Woods selected as his text Psalm 67, and he started his message by saying, "I would excite you by motives which no follower of Christ can resist, to make the spread of the gospel, and the conversion of the world, the object of your earnest and incessant pursuit." He went on to list as the motives for missionary concern: (1) the worth of souls; (2) the plenteous provision which Christ has made for their salvation; (3) the command of our Lord, "Go ye into all the world, and preach the gospel to every creature"; (4) the conduct of those who receive this command and of Christian missionaries in succeeding times; (5) the peculiar design of Christianity in contradistinction to Judaism and its adaptiveness to be a universal religion; (6) prophecy; (7) the operation of divine providence at the present time.

At the conclusion of his sermon Dr. Woods turned to the young missionaries who were the first to be sent out by any group in the United States and charged them in part as follows:

Dear Young Missionaries, I trust these feelings are yours. You have devoted your lives to the work of making known among the

Gentiles the unsearchable riches of Christ. We know you do not leave your native lande, because you have not the fairest prospect of reputation, usefulness, and comfort here. You go, we believe, because the love of God is shed abroad in your hearts by the Holy Ghost. We fondly look upon you, as chosen vessels unto Christ, to bear his name before the Gentiles. Blessed be the Lord God of the Gentiles, that he hath put this design into your hearts. The cause in which you have enlisted, is the cause of divine love. You have chosen the noblest and most honorable work on earth; more honorable than the laurels of conquerors, or the diadems of kings. But it is also arduous and perilous. Who is sufficient to do the work of an apostle to the heathen?

Then he turned to the whole congregation:

Brethren and friends, these dear young men are going to preach to the heathen that religion which is your comfort in life, your hope in death, your guide to heaven. Consider yourselves now looking upon them for the last time, before you shall meet them at the tribunal of Christ. Assist them in their arduous office by your substance and by your prayers. Bear them on your hearts when you draw near to God. The decisions of the judgment day will show, how cold has been our warmest zeal, how trifling our best exertions, how languid our most fervent prayers, compared to the greatness of the object now before us. The Lord of the universe, in these last days, is about to do a marvelous work; a work of astonishing power and grace. The time of his glory is come. He will soon destroy all idol worship. The thrones of wickedness he will level with the dust. He will dissipate the gross darkness which covers the nations. He will send out his light and truth, shed down his quickening Spirit, and renovate the world. The earth shall be full of the knowledge of the Lord, as the waters cover the sea.

The journeys of both the Judsons and Luther Rice on the separate ships were uneventful. At first the Judsons were plagued with seasickness, but once they became accustomed to the rolling waves, the journey proved to be an opportunity for study and meditation.

Adoniram Judson had been interested in a personal trans-

lation of the Greek New Testament into English while in the
seminary, and aboard the *Caravan* he continued his study with
particular emphasis on the word *baptizo*. The Congregationalist
Board of Commissioners had instructed him to baptize the
converts "and their households." He had wondered how he
would treat the children who might be included in the house-
hold but who might not be converted. He also felt that he must
be able to defend his position before the English Baptists who
were already in Calcutta. Ann Judson at first argued with her
husband over the controversial subject, but as she continued
her own private study she found herself in complete agreement. They made a further study in the library of the English
Baptists in Calcutta and finally were baptized at Serampore on
September 6, 1812, by William Ward, one of the English Baptist
missionaries, in the Lal Bazar Chapel in Calcutta. Ann Hasseltine wrote to her parents: "Thus, we are confirmed Baptists,
not because we wanted to be, but because truth compelled us
to be."

Luther Rice had arrived on the *Harmony* several weeks
later, but he, too, on November 1, was baptized and joined the
little Baptist church in Serampore.

Word had scarcely been able to reach the Congregationalist
Board of Commissioners and the Baptists in the United States
when the British East India Company ordered their deporta-
tion to England. Finally they secured their passage to the
Isle-de-France. After a seven-week sea journey, Luther Rice
had become ill and returned to the United States to regain his
health and to seek support for the new Baptist missionary
activity.

When news of the decisions made by Luther Rice and the
Judsons reached Boston, Dr. Thomas Baldwin, pastor of the
First Baptist Church, to whom Mr. Judson had written, called
a meeting of some of the leading Baptists of Massachusetts to
discuss the challenge which had been presented. He presented

Judson's letter which said, "Should there be formed a Baptist society for the support of a mission in these ports, I should be glad to consider myself their missionary." At this first meeting they formed the "Baptist Society for Propagating the Gospel in India and Other Foreign Parts." They wrote to the Judsons assuring them of their support.

Mission societies were also formed in Philadelphia, New York, Richmond, and other centers. When Luther Rice arrived in New York in September, he found a ready response in visits to Boston, New York, Philadelphia, Washington, Richmond, Charleston, and Savannah. He tells in his diary of a vision he had on the journey by carriage from Richmond to Petersburg of what Baptists in North America could do if they would only work together. Other men caught this vision and on May 18, 1814, thirty-three representatives, including eight laymen, some of whom had traveled three hundred miles by carriage, attended the meeting in the old First Baptist Church in Philadelphia "to elicit, combine, and direct the energies of the whole denomination."

The constitution was debated for six days and the major portion made the following provisions:

We, the delegated from the Missionary Societies, and other religious bodies of the Baptist denomination, in various parts of the United States, met in Convention, in the City of Philadelphia, for the purpose of carrying into effect the benevolent intentions of our constituents, by organizing a plan for eliciting, combining, and directing the energies of the whole denomination in one sacred effort for sending the glad tidings of Salvation to the heathen, and to nations destitute of pure Gospel light, Do AGREE to the following rules as fundamental principles, viz.:

I. That this body shall be styled "The General Missionary Convention of the Baptist Denomination in the United States of America for Foreign Missions."

II. That a Triennial Convention shall, hereafter, be held, consisting of Delegates, not exceeding two in number, from each of the several Missionary Societies, and other religious bodies of the Baptist denomination, now existing, or which may hereafter be formed in the United States, and which shall each regularly contribute to the general Missionary Fund, a sum amounting at least to one hundred dollars per annum.

III. That for the necessary transaction and dispatch of business, during the recess of the said Convention, there shall be a Board of twenty-one Commissioners, who shall be members of the said Societies, Churches, or other religious bodies aforesaid, triennially appointed by the said Convention, by ballot, to be called the "Baptist Board of Foreign Missions for the United States."

The first action taken by the newly organized Triennial Convention (so called because it met every three years) was the election of Luther Rice as representative and the election of the Judsons as missionaries.

In the meantime, the Judsons had landed in Rangoon, Burma, the first evangelical mission in modern times amid a hostile people. It was a capital crime in Burma for a native to forsake his ancestral religion. Six years passed before Moung Nau was baptized on June 27, 1819, as the first convert.

In the second meeting of the Triennial Convention in 1817, the delegates recognized the need for missions in the homeland as well as overseas. The dramatic story of this decision is recorded in the diary of John Mason Peck:

THURSDAY, 8TH. The convention heard the report of Brother Rice, their general agent. It was very interesting. Oh, how much does the zeal and activity of this devoted servant of the Redeemer reprove the slothfulness of others in this holy cause! Communications were then read from our brethren in India. Were it not for some particular circumstances, I should think it my duty to devote my life to that region. The Board made a report in part, in which they express their desire that a Western mission be entered upon.

FRIDAY, 9TH. Heard the further communications from Burma —a joint letter from Brethren Judson and Hough: their plan of missionary operations. They utter the Macedonian cry: "Come over and help us." They declare their intention never to give up the missionary cause. The Board recommended some necessary alterations in the constitution so as to embrace home missions; also to provide for the education of missionaries. . . .

TUESDAY, 13TH. After several important resolutions considered and adopted, the convention unanimously approved the doings of the Board for the three years past, censuring those individuals who have opposed and attempted to injure the mission. Next they took into consideration the subject of a mission to Africa; then heard the communications of two young men from Massachusetts (Coleman and Wheelock), who offer themselves to the Board. Their letters were very animating.

Received also a communication from New Orleans, setting forth the state of things in that region and the great, the pressing need of missionary labors. A Board for conducting the missions the next three years was then chosen. . . .

FRIDAY, 16TH. The Board still in session. Messrs. Coleman and Wheelock were accepted, and appointed missionaries to Rangoon. The subject of a domestic mission in the Southwest was brought forward. A letter from Rev. Mr. Ronaldson, of New Orleans, was read, and an appointment given him with the provision of five hundred dollars per annum for his support.

The business relating to myself was then brought forward. [He had presented a written document, fully explaining his views and feelings, offering himself as a candidate for appointment in the Western mission.]

The business was not taken up in a manner quite satisfactory to me; and the views of the Board seemed rather discordant on the question, *What should the Domestic Mission embrace?* Some seemed to entertain the idea that it must only embrace an itinerant mission among destitute churches and such places as are already Christianized. The business was finally deferred until tomorrow.

This view of the case brought a heavy trial on my mind. Indeed I see no way to obtain my object in the mission, but either to engage as a mere itinerant for a limited time, or to go exclusively among the Indians. The first I do not think my duty under existing circumstances; the last does not seem expedient. What will be the result I know not. But I feel to trust in a gracious God who will do all things well.

EVENING. Retired to rest, but slept little, on account of the agitation of my mind and the painful suspense under which I labored with regard to the mission.

SATURDAY, 17TH. This day, I suppose, will decide my future

prospects. How solemn the thought that a few hours must decide not only with respect to what I have been pursuing for two years past, but what relates to my whole life in the future! I feel a degree of resignation to the hand of God in whatever he may please to appoint. To *Him* will I commit the whole concern, believing that he will order what is best for his kingdom and glory. At ten o'clock met the Board of Missions. After some business of minor importance, Brother Welch made his communication to the Board. I made some further explanations, and then we withdrew. The decision is now pending. What will be the issue I know not.

SIX O'CLOCK. The long agony is over. The Board have accepted Mr. Welch and myself as missionaries to the Missouri Territory during our and their pleasure; and have appropriated the sum of one thousand dollars to defray our expenses in getting to St. Louis and for the support of the mission. In this I think I see the hand of God most visibly. From this moment I consider myself most sacredly devoted to the mission. O Lord, may I live and die in the cause!

LORD'S DAY, 18TH. Attended worship in the morning at Sansom Street. Reverend Daniel Sharp preached from Psalm cxix. 97, an excellent, eloquent, and appropriate discourse.

This day is one never to be forgotten. My fellow-laborer Welch and myself are to be solemnly set apart for the work of the mission. The exercises are to commence at five o'clock. It is a solemn consideration. I have now put my hand to the plow. O Lord, may I never turn back—never regret this step. It is my desire to live, to labor, to die as *a kind of pioneer* in advancing the gospel. I feel the most heavenly joy when my heart is engaged in this work.

2
Through Times of Tension

To some degree the seeds of tension, which ultimately led to the organization of the Southern Baptist Convention in 1845, were sown in the organization of the Triennial Convention in 1814. For the most part, the Baptists of New England were fiercely independent and were fearful of any ecclesiasticism or connectionalism. Rev. Daniel Sharp of Boston was the leader of the "society movement" and conceived of the societies in several of the larger cities uniting in their efforts. Dr. Thomas Baldwin of Boston, Dr. Richard Furman of Charleston, and Dr. W. B. Johnson were thinking more in terms of a national convention. This seems to have been the concept in the mind of Luther Rice; for he wrote to Adoniram Judson of a plan that had come to him while on a stagecoach journey from Richmond to Petersburg:

The plan which suggested itself to my mind, that of forming one principal society in each state, bearing the name of the state, and others in the same state auxiliary to that; and by these large, or state societies, delegates to be appointed to form one general society. . . . Several state conventions have been formed already, and more will probably be originated. To these, it is calculated, auxiliaries will be formed, and that associations will also become constituents; and that from there delegates, perhaps, ultimately, the delegates will be appointed to the general convention.

Between the organization of the Triennial Convention in 1814 and 1826 there was a struggle for supremacy of the society method or the convention method. By 1832 the American Baptist Home Mission Society had been formed and the society method had won supremacy. The Baptist Tract Society, now known as the American Baptist Publication Society, was organized in 1824.

Some of the southern states complained that more missionaries were sent by the Home Mission Society to northern and western states than to the South, and also some Baptists in the growing West felt that they were being neglected. This did not reflect an unconcern on the part of the mission society for these areas but represented an honest problem in obtaining personnel for pioneer work.

Starting in 1840, the fires of misunderstanding over slavery and the Abolitionist Movement spread and created suspicion on both sides. The Home Mission Society in 1841 had issued a circular setting forth its neutrality on the issue of appointing a slave holder as missionary. The General Foreign Mission Convention in April, 1844, had declared its neutrality, but the acting board in Boston told the Alabama Convention that it would not appoint a slave holder as a missionary. This led to the call of the Virginia Baptist Foreign Mission Society as follows:

To the Baptist Churches of Virginia and the Baptist Denomination of the United States generally:

Dear Brethren:

You will perceive by the accompanying resolutions of the Executive Committee of the Georgia Baptist Convention, that they have acceded to our proposal to hold in Augusta, Geo., on Thursday before the 2d Lord's day in May next, a Convention . . .

3. *Several important subjects,* besides the question of organizing a Foreign Mission Society, will, we presume, come under the consideration of the Convention. We will mention some of them, that our brethren in Virginia, especially, may learn, as far as practicable, the views and wishes of the denomination. Whether it will be better

to organize a separate Bible Society, and Publication Society, or to continue our connexion with the existing institutions, are questions which must be discussed. It is quite likely, too, that the subject of building up a common Southern Theological Institution will claim a share of attention.

JAMES B. TAYLOR, *Pres.*

Dr. W. W. Barnes in his history of the Southern Baptist Convention pointed out that the call issued from Virginia did not specify the character of the proposed organization; but Dr. W. B. Johnson, president of the South Carolina Convention and the first president of the Southern Baptist Convention, expressed his views favoring a convention-type of organization in a meeting of the South Carolina Convention at Edgefield the week before the meeting in Augusta.

Some Baptists thought in 1865, following the close of the War Between the States, there would be a reunion between the Northern and Southern Baptists. But Dr. Robert T. Baker in his book *Relations Between Northern and Southern Baptists* outlined some of the reasons why this reunion did not take place as follows: (1) preference for the "convention system" as over against the "society system"; (2) twenty years of separation in which the older men who had personal contacts had passed from the scene of action; (3) the bitterness of the sectional struggle during the war; (4) fear of too large an organization; (5) racial incidents and sociological differences; and (6) misunderstanding between Home Mission Society and Home Mission Board over procedure in working with Negroes and others in the South during the difficult days of reconstruction.

When it became apparent there was not to be a reunion, representatives of the two conventions met on September 12, 1894, in Fortress Monroe, Virginia, and reached agreement on three areas of work. The first two agreements had to do with co-operative work with Negro Baptists, while the third, which was submitted by the committee representing the Southern Baptist Convention, was favorably considered and referred to the Board of the American Baptist Home Mission Society. The proposition presented by the Southern Baptist Committee stated:

We believe that, for the promotion of fraternal feeling and of the best interest of the Redeemer's Kingdom, it is inexpedient for two different organizations of Baptists to solicit contributions or to establish missions in the same locality, and for this reason we recommend to the Home Mission Board of the Southern Baptist Convention and to the American Baptist Home Mission Society that, in the prosecution of their work already begun on contiguous fields or on the same field, all antagonisms be avoided, and that their officers and employees be instructed to co-operate in all practical ways in the spirit of Christ. That we further recommend to those bodies and their agents, in opening new work, to direct their efforts to localities not already occupied by the other.

The Fortress Monroe Agreement met its first big test with the division of Baptist churches in New Mexico. This followed the migration of many people from the South, and especially from Texas, into the New Mexico territory. On April 15, 1909, a conference was held in Washington, D. C., between representatives of the Home Mission Society and the Southern Baptist Convention, and it was agreed "that the Fortress Monroe agreement had expired and that its stipulations were not now in force or binding." However it was impossible to work out another agreement at this time, and tensions increased until representatives from the two general bodies hammered out some principles for further conference by the two groups represented and further refined in Hot Springs, Arkansas, January 24–25, 1912.

That statement of principles adopted by the committees or conference of the Northern and Southern Baptist Conventions stated:

It is unnecessary to review the last half century of denominational history. The possibilities of errors in judgment on the part of individuals or of missionary organizations is freely conceded. We must look to the future to correct the errors and failings of the past. We recognize the following as fundamental Baptist principles:

Fundamental Baptist Principles

1. The independence of the local Baptist church.
2. The moral interdependence and the co-operation of Baptist churches in promoting the interest of the Kingdom of God.
3. The purely advisory nature of all denominational organizations in their relations to Baptist churches.

Organizing Principles

1. The voluntary principles should rule in all general organizations among Baptists.
2. Contiguous Baptist churches should unite in district associations and in state conventions for the promotion of the Kingdom of God and their common denominational interest. The ideal organization is one association in a given territory and one convention in a given state. There may be local conditions, however, which make impracticable the immediate attainment of this ideal.

Concerning Comity

1. Financial aid given to churches by a general denominational body should create gratitude to God and promote Christian fraternity and service, but should not impair in any way the freedom of autonomy of the church or churches receiving such aid.
2. Denominational organizations of every kind should "jealously regard the rights of all sister organizations, and of the churches, being always careful to promote unity and harmony and to maintain inviolate the highest principles, thus exemplifying the noblest functions of liberty, to wit: a proper respect for the liberties of others."
3. No Baptist body should use its influence to disintegrate or injure the work of any other Baptist body. Every Baptist organization should be an integrating and constructive force.

Oklahoma Baptists voted single alignment with the Southern Baptist Convention in 1914 and the Missouri Baptist General Association voted single alignment in October, 1919, with the understanding that any persons or church preferring to co-operate with the Northern Baptist Convention could do so without censure.

With the coming of the dust bowl, the depression, and World War II, there was a tremendous turnover in population. For example, Oklahoma lost 301,900 by interstate civilian migration in the period from 1930 to 1940, and more than 303,000 during the early days of World War II from April, 1940, to November, 1943. North Carolina lost nearly 63,000 in the depression decade and more than 250,000 from 1940 to 1943. Kentucky had a similar loss, and Arkansas lost more than 100,000 in the decade from 1930 to 1940 and 250,000 in the first three years of the 1940 decade. These four Southern states lost more during this thirteen-year period than any other states in the United States. Mississippi, South Carolina, Georgia, Missouri, and Alabama joined these four in substantial losses during this period of time.

The destination of many of these civilian migrants can be seen when you note that California led by a tremendous margin with more than 1,000,000 net balance during the decade from 1930 to 1940 and an additional 1,350,000 during the first three years of the 1940 decade. Michigan, Washington, and Ohio were among the first five in net gain during the period from 1940 to 1943. It is significant to note that this tremendous sociological change in our population occurred either during the depression years when it was impossible for any churches to do much building of new churches or mission points because of the financial condition, or during the early war years when it was impossible to obtain materials.

On May 10, 1936, sixteen Baptists who had been members of Southern Baptist churches, mostly in Oklahoma and Arkansas, met and organized the First Southern Baptist Church in Shafter, California. Four churches which had been organized formed an association in 1939 and on September 13, 1940, messengers from thirteen churches met and organized the Southern Baptist General Convention of California. At the meeting of the Southern Baptist Convention in Birmingham, Alabama, in 1941, a petition was presented by the new convention for recognition as a co-operating constituency. A committee was appointed to study the matter, and at the meeting of the Southern Baptist Convention in San Antonio in 1942 the committee asked that it be continued for another year, but a minority report which called for immediate recognition of California was adopted.

Dr. Blake Smith, pastor of the University Baptist Church, Austin, Texas, presented a very helpful discussion of American and Southern Baptist relations before the ministers' council of the American Baptist Convention in 1959, which was later published in the *Crusader*. Dr. Smith outlined many of the factors which led to the tensions developing in the 1940's, but he overlooked one significant factor which was presented to the Southern Baptist Convention in San Antonio and which had great influence in the decision of the Convention to adopt the minority report presented by Dr. J. B. Rounds at that time. The Northern Baptist Convention at Atlantic City on May 25, 1940, adopted the following resolution: "*Resolved*, That the Northern Baptist Convention direct its General Council to make inquiries, and if desirable, to authorize conversations with a responsible body from the Disciples of Christ to explore possibilities and difficulties that would result from closer conference understanding and co-operation between the two denominations." These conversations between the Northern Baptists and the Disciples of Christ continued until 1952.

In 1949 when the Northern Baptist Convention first considered the matter of a change of name to the American Baptist Convention, it was also voted "in conformity with the remarks of the chairman of the commission of review, to invite the Southern Baptist Convention to unite with us in the American

Baptist Convention." In the same year the special committee on conference with Southern Baptists was discharged, and the action of the 1949 convention was never communicated to the Southern Baptist Convention. A resolution was adopted in 1950 by the Northern Baptist Convention "affirming as we adopt the name American Baptist Convention that we hold the name in trust by all Christians of like faith and mind who desire to bear witness to the historic Baptist convictions in a framework of co-operative protestantism."

During this period from 1940 to 1950, communications were on a polite but cool basis. A joint committee urged in 1948 "a new spirit of mutual understanding and appreciation between Northern and Southern Baptists. After hours of conference and investigation, we find that a large majority in both conventions agree, to an encouraging extent, in fundamental Baptist principles. We find, likewise, that in some cases where criticism has arisen, it has come from personality rather than principle. It is our conviction, that, since we have so much in common as Baptists, we should exercise a spirit of Christian charity at the point at which we differ without compromise of the principles of either convention."

Reaction among Southern Baptists is demonstrated by the report of the committee to discuss common problems with Northern Baptists which was adopted in 1949 as follows:

First: Resolved That, because local Baptist churches are independent in nature, they may be organized by Baptists anywhere with or without reference to grievances of other Baptist churches, or any other religious body. This liberty, of course, should never be used as a license to injure the work of other bodies.

Second: Resolved That, because of the voluntary principles that prevail, churches, associations, and state conventions of Baptists may co-operate with whomsoever they will, irrespective of geographical location.

Third: Resolved That, because of moral interdependence of Baptist bodies, co-operation should take place wherever possible between all Baptist individuals, churches, associations, and conventions. The general denominational bodies, furthermore, should themselves strive for mutual good will and understanding. This does not mean deviation from conviction, but recognizes that the Christian task is larger than any segment of its followers. The application of these principles as set out in the foregoing three resolutions, as a matter of fact, have already been exhibited in the acceptance by the Southern Baptist Convention, meeting in San Antonio in 1942, of Baptists in California, and at Memphis in 1948, of Baptists in Kansas.

Fourth: Be It Further *Resolved* That, no compact or agreement be formed with any organization, convention, or religious body that would place Southern Baptists in a compromising position, or would appear to be a step toward organic union with religious bodies that do not believe in or practice the aforesaid New Testament Baptist principles as set out in this report.

At the meeting of the Executive Committee of the Baptist World Alliance in September, 1954, Dr. Reuben Nelson, the general secretary of the American Baptist Convention, and Dr. V. C. Hargroves, then president of the American Baptist Convention, asked for a conference with representatives from the Southern Baptist Convention dealing with points of tension between the two groups. A further conference was arranged for January 20, 1955, in Washington, D. C., with Dr. Nelson, Dr. Hargroves, Dr. C. Oscar Johnson, Dr. Ralph Johnson, Dr. Courts Redford, Dr. James L. Sullivan, Dr. C. C. Warren, Dr. Sydnor Stealey, Dr. Porter Routh, along with the secretaries of the state conventions for both American Baptists and Southern Baptists in Ohio and Illinois, and several others. There was a frank and free discussion by those involved, and these informal recommendations were adopted:

1. That we recognize also that there are some things about which we conscientiously differ and that we continue our prayerful efforts to understand each other.
2. That conferences of local, state, and national leaders be held in

areas where advisable and mutually desired by all conventions involved.

3. That conferences of convention leaders and groups be continued in an effort to explore and discover areas of co-operation.

4. That a concerted effort by local leaders and representatives of both conventions be made to correct unjustifiable criticism which is causing misunderstanding among us.

5. That we strive for a greater degree of co-operation in the matter of the location of churches.

6. That we encourage the leaders of the two conventions to consider the adoption of some common goals and long-range objectives such as might relate to evangelism, stewardship, Christian education, and the celebration of the sesquicentennial of the Triennial Convention.

7. That we make this whole matter of co-operation an object of earnest prayer and maintain the faith that we can learn more about going together in winning America and the world to Christ.

The spirit of this conference was communicated by Dr. C. C. Warren, then chairman of the Executive Committee of the Southern Baptist Convention, to Dr. Guy Moore, chairman of the Convention's committee on world evangelism. This committee recommended to Southern Baptists in May, 1955, "that we call upon our Home Mission Board's Department of Evangelism to seek a plan whereby we can co-operate with our Baptist bodies such as the American Baptist Convention, the Negro Baptist Conventions, etc., in a great nation-wide evangelistic crusade or emphasis during the year 1958 or 1959— and that we call upon the Executive Committee of our Convention to confer with the various agencies of the Southern Baptist Convention and with representatives of our Baptist conventions in North America, looking toward the announcement in 1959 of a five-year program of advance which will culminate in 1964, the date of the one-hundred-fiftieth anniversary of the organization of Baptist work on a national level in the United States and North America."

The American Baptist Convention responded to this action by the Southern Baptist Convention and representatives from

many Baptist groups attended the first organization conference
at the Conrad Hilton Hotel in Chicago on December 8, 1955.
This conference discussed many of the problems involved in
relationships and adopted the following motion:

That in view of the actions taken by the Southern Baptist Convention, the American Baptist Convention, and the National Baptist
Convention of U.S.A., Inc., (1) we approve in principle a great co-
operative program of witness and work by our Baptist bodies in the
United States, 1959–1964, leading up to a worthy celebration in
1964 of the Third Jubilee or one-hundred-fiftieth anniversary of
organized Baptist work on a national level; (2) we recommend consideration by the participating groups of the following schedule of
emphases:

> 1959—Evangelism
> 1960—Bible Teaching and Baptist Witness
> 1961—Stewardship and Enlistment
> 1962—Church Extension and Leadership Training
> 1963—World Missions
> 1964—Third Jubilee

It was against this background that the seven bodies working together in the Jubilee Advance adopted the following
statement in 1958:

Seven North American Baptist bodies, differing conscientiously
in some areas of policy and practice, have banded themselves together in the Baptist Jubilee Advance, for the purpose of fellowship,
mutual aid, shared objectives, and a common passion for the redemption of men.

In this Baptist Jubilee Advance each co-operating unit desires
and prays for the strengthening and advance of brother Baptists of
other bodies and areas. None desires to grow at the expense of
others; none believes it has the right to say to another, "We must increase and you should decrease."

Each believes that where one member of the body rejoices, all
the members rejoice with it. Each believes that Baptist advance in
North America should be an advance on every convention and conference front. Each co-operating unit would use its distinctive or-

ganization and its particular methods and resources. Each will strive for the enlargement of its particular fellowship in the faith. But this spirit-prompted ambition will not tolerate scorn of any brethren, or that type of rivalry which flaunts the principle of brotherhood.

It cannot be denied that unhappy tensions have at times barred relationships among Baptist bodies in North America, even when these bodies have affirmed their oneness in things essential and their membership in one great world family of Baptists. Neither can it be denied that at times one or another body has appeared to ignore the rights, feelings and best interests of fellow Baptists, even though such practice has at times resulted from preoccupation with unilateral concerns. . . .

Members of the various Baptist Jubilee Advance committees are of one mind in the conviction that all North American Baptists need a deepening of devotion to Jesus Christ, a quickening of evangelistic zeal, a worthier level of stewardship, and a more vital and fruitful church life. To advance together in these areas of humbling challenge is our earnest hope. To establish many needed Baptist churches in all parts of this continent and its growing population and its multitude of people outside the fold of Christ is the responsibility of all bodies united for fellowship in action within the Baptist Jubilee Advance. Not as competitors, but as compatriots; not in fear of one another, but with deeper faith in one another; not with jealousy, but with shared joy, Baptists of North America should march forward toward a nobler destiny.

In conclusion it must be admitted that there are still areas of discussion which need to be considered. The editorials presented by Baptist editors both in the American Convention and in the Southern Baptist Convention recognize this fact. It should be noted, however, that there are already channels through which discussions can take place. Helpful discussions on the particular problem level have taken place during the past few years between representatives of the two Negro conventions and the Southern Baptist Convention. This conference has been enlarged to include the American Baptists for the discussion of common educational problems with the Negro Baptist conventions. Plans are being made to continue the

channels through some organization after the conclusion of
the Baptist Jubilee Advance, perhaps under the leadership of
the Baptist World Alliance.

Good communications involves both a stimulus and a response. There are opportunities for both in the present relationships.

3

Organized for Action

Relationships and co-operation have long been areas of interests in New Testament churches. Our polity should be consistent with a scriptural basis. It has developed to meet certain needs. This development constantly needs evaluation in the face of historical tradition or continuity, and also in the face of the challenge of a new day.

First, it might be well to examine the New Testament church to discover how it was governed. What was its relationship with other churches? How did it meet the opportunities of its day?

One of the phenomena of the early Christian movement was the speed with which the gospel was taken to the great urban centers of the Roman Empire. These churches had a common Saviour, but they had differences according to the evangelists who first preached there, the nature and occupation of the people and their culture. We know that Jerusalem was largely a Jewish church under the leadership of James. It took pride in its background. It viewed with alarm and suspicion the entry of those who had not conformed to Jewish tradition on equal terms. Philip founded the church at Caesarea and it became a center of a liberal Gentile Christianity. The church at Antioch had a cosmopolitan character and the influence of Paul and Peter gave it a missionary and outward-looking character. The Greek influence was felt in Ephesus where Paul had such a tremendous influence. The church at Rome

was another cosmopolitan church and had different charac-
teristics.

Against these varying backgrounds, it was natural that there
should be some differences in their organization. For example,
the church at Jerusalem followed to some degree the lines of
the Jewish synagogue which had a board of presbyters who
constituted a committee for management. It was here that the
office of deacon arose.

At Antioch the five leaders of the church were called
prophets and teachers, and there seems to have been a corporate vote in sending out Barnabas and Paul. There seems to
have been some shifting in the emphasis of Paul in the organization of the church in his letter to the Corinthians: "Within
our community God has appointed, in the first place apostles,
in the second place prophets, thirdly teachers; then miracle-
workers, then those who have gifts of healing, or ability to
help others or power to guide them, or the gift of ecstatic
utterance of various kinds" (1 Cor. 12:28, *The New English
Bible*). He wrote to the Ephesians: "These were his gifts:
some to be apostles, some prophets, some evangelists, some
pastors and teachers, to equip God's people for work in his
service, to the building up of the body of Christ" (4:11–12,
The New English Bible). We find a varying list of church
officers from those reported by Luke in Acts 20:17, *The New
English Bible:* "He did, however, send from Miletus to Ephesus
and summon the elders of the congregation."

One thing seems to be clear: there was no uniform pattern
imposed on the churches and they seemed to be free to do as
they needed. This does not mean that the emphasis is on
independence as over against unity in Christ, but it does
indicate as far as church government was concerned there was
to be found freedom—under the lordship of Jesus Christ.

There are some differences in organization among Baptist
groups in North America. There are many points of similarity.

All recognize the independence of the local church. All have associational organizations. All depend on the voluntary stewardship of members and churches for support.

Misunderstandings grow out of ignorance rather than knowledge. The brief review of the organizations utilized by the 77,000 churches co-operating in the Baptist Jubilee is presented in the hope that knowledge will motivate interest and understanding.

American Baptist Convention

The Northern Baptist Convention was organized in 1907 and changed its name to the American Baptist Convention in 1950.

The first Baptist co-operative organization in the United States was the Philadelphia Association organized in 1707. The conversion of Adoniram Judson and Luther Rice to the Baptist position in 1813 led to the formation in 1814 of the General Missionary Convention of the Baptist Denomination in the United States for Foreign Missions. This organization expressed concern for both foreign missions and home missions in the early days of its being but later concentrated on foreign missions. It is now recognized as the American Baptist Foreign Missions Society. The Baptist General Tract Society was formed in 1824 and is now the American Baptist Publication Society. The American Baptist Home Mission Society refers to 1832 as its beginning. Later the American Baptist Historical Society was started in 1852, the Woman's American Baptist Foreign Mission Society in 1871, the Woman's American Baptist Home Mission Society in 1877, and the American Baptist Education Society in 1888. The Ministers and Missionaries Benefit Board was organized in 1911.

The American Baptist societies were all autonomous, and members generally came together in May for the annual meeting at some central place. It was out of the "May meeting" of these various societies that a call for a convention was issued in

1906; it was held in connection with the May anniversaries in Washington, D. C., in 1907. A committee of fifteen was selected to draft a plan which would provide for some co-ordination but also preserve the independence of the local church. Charles Evans Hughes, later chief justice of the United States Supreme Court, was elected as the first president. The Convention was chartered by the state of New York in 1910 "to give expression to the opinions of its constituency upon moral, religious, and denominational matters, and to promote denominational unity and efficiency in efforts for the evangelization of the world." In its opening declaration the Convention stated: "The American Baptist Convention declares its belief in the independence of the local church, and in the purely advisory nature of all denominational organizations composed of representatives of churches. It believes also that, in view of the growth of the Baptist denomination and its extension throughout our country, there is need for an organization to serve the common interest of the entire denomination as state and district organizations serve their respected constituencies."

The constitution of the American Baptist Convention provides that "the constituency of the American Baptist Convention shall be all Baptist churches in the United States which co-operate in its work." The American Baptist Convention considers Puerto Rico as a state convention. The Convention provides that each church may appoint two delegates and also any "missionary members on furlough so appointed who have been duly commissioned and who are approved by their respected society." It provides for one additional delegate for every one hundred members above the first one hundred with the provision that the maximum ratio will be in keeping with "the amount of benevolence funds given by or through the same church during the same period."

The constitution of the American Baptist Convention also

provides that "accredited officers and members of the Board of Managers of each of the co-operating organizations and the Ministers and Missionaries Benefit Board and the Board of Education as well as officers and members of committees, councils, commissions, and other similar authorized groups of the Convention" shall automatically be voting members.

The officers of the American Baptist Convention are president, first and second vice-president, general secretary, and treasurer. All officers are elected for one-year terms with the exception of the general secretary, who is elected for a three-year term, and who is the "principle administrative officer of the Convention and of the General Council." The General Council is made up of the officers of the Convention, the immediate past president, and thirty-six members elected by the Convention, including laymen, women, and ministers. Executives of agencies, state conventions, and city societies are associate members but without vote.

Offices for the American Baptist Convention are located in Valley Forge, Pennsylvania.

Funds for the general support of missions in the American Baptist Convention generally are sent to the national offices, and the allocations to the states and the city societies are worked out of the national organization.

At one time separate organizations for the operation of mission programs at home and overseas were maintained by both the convention and the women's organization, but both of these are now carried on as joint operations. The American Baptist Foreign Mission Society still carries on work in Burma.

Canadian Baptist Federation

Baptist churches were first organized in Canada during the middle of the eighteenth century, with the first members coming from New England and later members arriving from Scotland and England.

The first Baptist church in Canada was organized in 1763 in Wolfville, Nova Scotia, under the leadership of Ebenezer Moulton, a Baptist pastor who had come from Massachusetts. Other pastors came into the Maritime Provinces, and in 1800 many of the younger churches came together to organize the Nova Scotia Baptist Association. The Baptist Convention of Nova Scotia, New Brunswick, and Prince Edward Island was formed in 1846.

Another group of Baptists from New England in the Maritime Provinces was known as the "Free Baptists," and conversations between the two groups started in 1884. The United Baptist Convention of the Maritime Provinces was created in 1906. During and after the American Revolution, thousands of loyalists moved across the Canadian border to continue living under the British flag. Most of these were members of the Anglican church, but some were Baptists and helped to strengthen the work in the Maritimes and also in Lower and Upper Canada. Caldwell's Manor Church was started in Quebec as early as 1796. Work soon started in Ottawa Valley with Baptists from Scotland, and one of the leaders in the growth of the work was a pioneer minister, Daniel McPhail, who was pastor at Osgoode for twenty-six years and became known as the "Elijah of the Ottawa Valley."

A young Swiss widow, Madame Henriette Feller, came to St. Johns, Quebec, in 1835 and started a school and church among the French Canadians. This was the start of the Grande Ligne Mission with its affiliated French Baptist churches. The Baptist Convention of Ontario and Quebec was created in 1889.

Baptists of Ontario and Quebec sent missionaries to the West as early as 1869 and organized the first church in Winnipeg in 1875, and the first Baptist church west of the Rockies in Victoria in 1876. The Baptist Union of Western Canada was formed in 1907.

At the close of 1962 there were about 1,300 churches in the

three Canadian conventions with about 150,000 members. There are ten associations in the Maritimes, nineteen in Ontario and Quebec, and seven in the West.

The Canadian Baptist Federation, which is made up of all three conventions, grew out of the need for a national organization which would include all of the churches. The Canadian Baptist Foreign Mission Board was established in 1911, the Women's Dominion Committee in 1935, and the Baptist Publication Committee of Canada was organized in 1937. The Federation came into existence at a meeting in St. Johns, New Brunswick, in 1944. The objective of the Federation as stated in the constitution is

to afford opportunities for consultation, study and united policy-making and action, on questions affecting the welfare of the churches, the support and accrediting of the ministry, and the extension of the church both at home and abroad. This consultation and policy-making should include home missions, foreign missions, Grande Ligne, education, ministerial training and credentials, superannuation, social service, evangelism, Sunday school and young people's work, the publication of religious literature, and any other matters of common interest and urgency. Administrative action shall, however, rest with the regional conventions, the association or the churches; although, where the matter has been decided by general consent, more specifically united action may always be taken by the whole denomination in any phase of its work.

The Federation does not elect the trustees for the general boards nor does it have the responsibility of raising money from the churches. This responsibility is assigned to the area conventions. The Federation is authorized to have a special Federation Day for the raising of funds, but the over-all budget is underwritten by the three conventions.

The National Baptist Conventions

Both the National Baptist Convention of America and the National Baptist Convention of U.S.A., Inc. refer to 1880, when the Foreign Mission Convention of Negro Baptists was organized, as the starting point for their conventions. The actual convention of the National Baptists of America was not organized until 1886 following an open letter to the Baptist clergy issued by William J. Simmons in which he submitted the following reasons for its organization:

1. To promote personal piety, sociability, and a better knowledge of each other.
2. To be able to have an understanding as to the great ends to be reached by the denomination.
3. To encourage our literary men and women, and promote the interest of Baptist literature.
4. To discuss questions pertaining especially to the religious, educational, industrial, and social interests of our people.
5. To give an opportunity for the best thinkers and writers to be heard.
6. That, united, we may be more powerful for good and strengthen our pride in the denomination.

The National Baptist Convention continued as one organization until 1915, when a misunderstanding over the publishing board led to the division and the organization of the National Baptist Convention of America and the National Baptist Convention, U.S.A., Inc.

National Baptists of America

The constitution of this Convention states its nature and function as follows: "The National Baptist Convention of America shall serve as an agency of Christian education, missionary and church extension; and combine the efforts of Baptist churches and organizations in extending the gospel both at home and to the foreign fields; and propagate Baptist doctrines of faith and distinctive principles throughout the world." Its aim is to "give its influence in maintaining and safeguarding full religious liberty and spiritual independence on both the home and foreign fields."

Memberships in their annual conventions are provided on a church, association, and state convention basis. Each church which registers with a minimum of $25.00 is entitled to one messenger, with $10.00 for each additional messenger. Each association which pays $50.00 is entitled to two messengers, with $10.00 for each additional messenger, and each state convention which pays $100 is entitled to five messengers with $10.00 for each additional messenger.

The Convention further provides for an executive board which consists of the elected officers of the Convention, the chairman and corresponding secretaries of the board, and the presidents of the state conventions. The executive board is empowered to transact any unfinished business of the Convention, to arrange for regional meetings and conferences, and to change the site of the convention.

The president of the National Baptist Convention serves as the chairman of the executive board and is authorized to call regular and special meetings and to sign all orders drawn on the treasurer. He also has the responsibility of appointing all committees and commissions not elected by the Convention.

The National Baptist Convention lists seven boards in its organization made up of one member from each state convention and general association, and approved by the convention. These boards are the Home Mission Board, Foreign Mission Board, BTU Board, National Baptist Publishing Board, Evangelical Board, Benevolent Board, and Educational Board. The chairman, corresponding secretary, and three other members of the board constitute the board of management. The boards must report to the Convention and are "subject to the convention in all it does during the meeting of the convention and during the interims." Compensation of each officer and employee is fixed by the board, but compensation is limited to the chairman, recording secretary, and corresponding secretary.

In addition to the Convention itself there is a Senior Woman's Auxiliary National Baptist Convention, a Junior Woman's Auxiliary, a National Baptist Brotherhood Auxiliary Convention, and the Nurses' Corps of the National Baptist Convention. All messengers to these auxiliary conventions must be appointed and certified by their churches, and the auxiliary conventions are subject to the action of the National Baptist Convention. The auxiliary conventions are required to report all of their receipts and disbursements to the National Convention and "under no circumstances" shall the expense "exceed 40 per cent of the total raise." The auxiliary conventions are authorized to accept representation fees from any and all auxiliaries of the local church included in their work, subject to their approved constitutional regulations.

The National Baptist Convention of America does not have any regular week-by-week or month-by-month plan of financial support similar to the Cooperative Program, and much of the money is raised in connection with the meeting of the National Convention.

The National Baptist Convention seeks to maintain confidence in its financial system by the proper use of receipts and reports which are made to the Convention and published in its annual proceedings. The Convention guarantees that all designated funds must go to the cause for which they are designated, and the Convention allocates only undesignated funds.

The denomination publishes through its Publishing Board *The Union-Review,* the denominational paper which provides a channel of communication for the president and promotion of the various phases of work of the national organization. Some idea of the scope of the work of the Publishing Board is demonstrated by the fact that its receipts for the year closing June 30, 1961, amounted to $783,000, with disbursements during the same period amounting to $715,000. The net worth of the National Baptist Publishing Board is listed at nearly a million dollars.

Schools endorsed by the National Baptist Convention of America include: Mary Allen College, Crockett, Texas; Conroe Normal and Industrial College, Conroe, Texas; Easonian Baptist Seminary, Birmingham, Alabama; Morris College, Sumter, South Carolina; Union Baptist Seminary, New Orleans, Louisiana; Guadalupe College, Seguin, Texas; Liberty Baptist College, Muskogee, Oklahoma; Florida Normal and Industrial College, St. Augustine, Florida; Mississippi Baptist Seminary, Hattiesburg, Mississippi.

As the National Baptist Convention grew out of a missionary convention, it continues in its foreign mission interest to this day. During a recent year it reported income of more than $60,000 and supported mission work in Africa, in Haiti, and in Panama. The Foreign Mission Board also assisted foreign students in their study in the United States.

National Baptists, U.S.A., Inc.

The object of the National Baptist Convention, United States of America, Incorporated, is: "To promote home and foreign missions; to encourage and support Christian education; to publish and distribute Sunday school and other religious literature; and to engage in whatever other Christian endeavor is required to advance the Redeemer's kingdom throughout the world."

Representation in the Convention is provided on basis of churches, associations, district conventions, and state conventions, "all known to be in harmony with the purpose of this convention." For example, churches with two hundred to five hundred members must pay $25.00 for representation, churches with five hundred to one thousand members $35.00, churches above one thousand members $50.00, and churches with less than two hundred members $10.00. Each church is allowed an additional messenger for each $10.00 paid, but no church is allowed more than ten messengers.

State conventions are allowed representation on the basis of $200 paid, with an additional messenger for each $50.00, but no state may have more than two messengers. The district convention pays $50.00 for representation and the association $35.00. In addition, the constitution provides, "Any person who is in good and regular standing in any missionary Baptist church that is a member of this convention, may become a life member by the payment of the sum of $200 into the treasury of this convention."

The National Baptist Convention, U.S.A., Inc., provides for a board of directors which consists of the president, the vice-president at large, the four regional vice-presidents, and the vice-presidents elected by the Convention from the various states and territories represented at the annual convention. Other members are the secretary, the treasurer, the attorney, the editor, historiographer, statistician, the assistant secretaries of the Convention, and fifteen members at large to be elected by the Convention annually. The board of directors elects its own chairman and secretary and is authorized to set up such subcommittees as it may deem proper. The board of directors is authorized "to complete the unfinished business of the convention; and to adjust such matters as may be referred to it by the convention and fill any vacancies which may occur in the roster of the convention, to nominate and fix the time and place of the meeting; to enforce the orders of the convention or any of its boards; to examine and pass on, and recommend all claims against the convention; and during the recess of the convention have entire charge of its affairs."

At the present time the National Baptist Convention, U.S.A., Inc., has a Foreign Mission Board, Home Mission Board, Sunday School Publishing Board, BTU Board, Education Board, Ministerial Benefit Board, and Moderators' Auxiliary.

Besides its boards, the National Baptist Convention, U.S.A., Inc., recognized as subsidiary bodies the Woman's Convention, auxiliary to the National Baptist Convention; Sunday School and BTU Congress; and the Baptist Layman's Movement. It is provided that these subsidiary bodies shall make annual reports to the Convention and their reports are subject to the approval of the Convention.

The National Baptist Convention Sunday School Publishing Board reported total sales for the year June 30, 1960, of $984,989, with net earnings of $63,736. This office, located in Nashville, Tennessee, not only publishes the Sunday school literature for many National Baptist Convention churches, but also publishes *The Voice*, which is the publication of the National Baptist Convention.

The National Baptist Training Union Board provides the literature for the Training Union in the National Baptist churches. They reported total sales of $149,866 and contributed $5,000 in the year closing June 30, 1960, to the ministerial retirement fund.

North American Baptist General Conference

The North American Baptist General Conference finds its background out of a stream of events which began in 1814, the same year the Triennial Convention was organized. In that year a Scotch merchant came to Varel in the Grand Duchy of Oldenburg to collect on goods smuggled into Germany during Napoleon's blockade. He met a fourteen-year-old lad by the name of Johann Gerhard Oncken and gave the boy a Bible. Although Oncken had been confirmed as a Lutheran, he started reading the Bible and soon became an earnest soul-winning Christian. He moved to Hamburg, Germany, and without any contact with Baptists, he came to the conviction of believer's baptism. He met Professor Barnas Sears, an American Baptist taking work at the University of Halle.

German Baptists take great delight today in pointing to the spot on the Elbe River where Oncken and six others were baptized under cover of darkness on April 22, 1834, and organized the first Baptist church in Germany. One of those seven, a cobbler by the name of H. J. Krueger, became the founder of the North American Baptist Church in Peoria, Illinois. Many Germans who fled persecution in their homeland to come to America were baptized by Oncken.

Another seed was planted when a young Christian handed Anton Konrad Fleischmann a tract as he was crossing Lake Geneva in Switzerland. A further study of the Bible convinced him on believer's baptism, and in Newark, New Jersey, in 1839, he started preaching the message of conversion, regeneration, and Christian living. Because he refused to christen babies, he moved to Pennsylvania, where a great revival resulted in his preaching in and near Philadelphia. On March 20, 1843, Fleischmann baptized five persons, and on July 9, they signed the statement of faith drawn up by himself and constituted themselves as members of "The German Church of the Lord that Meets on Poplar Street." This is recognized as the oldest church in the North American Baptist General Conference today.

At the time the Southern Baptist Convention was organized in 1845, there were a dozen or more German Baptist churches covering a wide area in North America. Through the Publication Society and the Home Mission Society of the American Baptist Convention, they became conscious of one another, and the first conference was held in 1851 in Philadelphia. Participating churches were located in Newark, New Jersey; New York City; Rochester and Buffalo, New York; Philadelphia, Pennsylvania; St. Louis, Missouri; Chicago, Illinois; and Bridgeport, Ontario. Other churches not affiliated in the original meeting had been organized in Indiana, Wisconsin, in Cincinnati, Ohio, and Pittsburgh, Pennsylvania. After a sea-son of prayer, the conference was opened by singing, "Ach bleib mit deiner gnade bei uns, Herr Jesu Christ," "The Lord Be with Us as Each Day His Blessings We Receive." This is a song which has been dear to the hearts of German Baptists through the years as a prayer to the Lord Jesus Christ to abide with his grace.

Dr. O. E. Krueger, in writing of this first meeting in *In God's Hand*, said:

They believed the Bible to be the only and fully adequate guide in faith and practice. Under the illumination of the Holy Spirit, everyone has the right of interpreting the Bible for himself. Every church stands upon the authority of the Lord Jesus Christ. No pope, bishop, or synod can dictate to the local church. Every church must be composed of regenerated members who have confessed the Lord in baptism. Infant baptism and confirmation do not make a person a Christian.

A church cannot consist of a mixed membership, that is to say, part believers and part non-believers. They insisted on a manner of Christian life patterned after that of Jesus, whom they accepted as Saviour, Lord, and example. The hand of fellowship must be withdrawn from those who fail to accept that standard of life. The conferences were to be conferences, pure and simple, without legislative power over the local church.

Churches related to the North American Baptist General Conference now report more than fifty-two thousand members with more than three hundred churches. Something of their sense of dedication is reflected in the fact that the per-member contribution in 1961 was $111.33 compared with $68.96 for American Baptists and $50.24 for Southern Baptists.

The North American Baptist General Conference meets every two years, and its headquarters are located at 7308 Madison Street in Forest Park, Illinois. The General Council is made up of men selected by the North American Baptist General Conference and has general oversight of the cooperative work of the Conference.

The home mission as well as the foreign mission work of the North American Baptist General Conference is carried on through the General Missionary Society.

One phase of their mission work is church extension, and in 1962 they reported forty-four churches receiving mission aid. Another phase of the mission work is among the Indians of Saskatchewan and Alberta, Canada. North American Baptists have also carried on some Spanish American missions in Colorado and Texas. They support nine missionaries in four stations in Japan and co-operate with the Osaka Biblical Seminary. One of their largest missionary thrusts is the Cameroon Mission in West Africa.

Other departments of work carried on by the North American Baptist General Conference are evangelism and church extension, stewardship and higher education, as well as the work of the Department of Christian Education, Woman's Missionary Union, North American Baptist Men, the Ministers' Fellowship, and the Publication Society. The two publications are the *Baptist Herald* and *Der Sendbote*.

The two schools which are supported are the North American Baptist Seminary at Sioux Falls, South Dakota, and the Christian Training Institute at Edmonton, Alberta.

Seventh-Day Baptists

Shortly after the organization of the first Baptist church in England, there was organized the Seventh-Day Baptist Church of Mill Yard, Goodman's Field, in London. It probably was organized in 1607 by Mr. and Mrs. John Trask, and its membership once included Dr. Peter Chamberlin, a royal physician to three kings and queens. Another member was John James, who was put to death because of his belief in the sabbath, and Nathaniel Bailey, the author of *Bailey's Dictionary*, one of the earliest dictionaries published.

The first Seventh-Day Baptist Church in America was organized at Newport, Rhode Island, in 1671. In 1664 Stephen Mumford, an English Seventh-Day Baptist, had come to America and settled at Newport, Rhode Island. He led other members of the Baptist church there to accept his views on the sabbath, and the organization of the church followed. A Seventh-Day Baptist minister, Abel Noble, came to near Philadelphia from England in 1684. Between that date and 1700 a dozen churches of that persuasion were organized in the neighborhood.

The Piscataway Seventh-Day Baptist Church in New Jersey was organized in 1705 after Edmund Dunham started observing the sabbath day. From these beginnings have come other churches until there are now nearly seventy churches in the United States with a total membership of nearly six thousand.

Even before the Triennial Convention was organized in 1814, the Seventh-Day Baptist General Conference was organized in 1801. The General Conference has annual meetings and is divided into nine associations for regional fellowship.

The *Guide to Church Membership* published by the Seventh-Day Baptists Board of Christian Education says:

The General Conference works through several boards and agencies. One of these is the Missionary Society, which was organized in 1818. This agency conducts missionary work in several foreign countries, including Nyasaland (Africa), Jamaica, and British Guiana, and also in this country. The American Sabbath Tract Society, another agency, was founded in 1835. It publishes the *Sabbath Recorder*, a weekly magazine, and tracts telling about our denomination and beliefs. It also controls the Seventh-Day Baptist Publishing House, called the Recorder Press, located in Plainfield, New Jersey. The Board of Christian Education is responsible for sabbath school publications and helps in the religious educational work throughout the denomination. The Historical Society was organized in 1916, and is located in the Seventh-Day Building at Plainfield, New Jersey, where a museum of historical interest is kept. The Woman's Society is responsible for work of special interest to the women of the denomination. The Memorial Board has charge of the Memorial Fund, which provides an income for various activities of the General Conference. This fund totaled $1,117,351 in May, 1959.

Three colleges existing today were started by Seventh-Day Baptists: Alfred University, Alfred, New York; Milton College, Milton, Wisconsin; and Salem College, Salem, West Virginia. Special training for our ministers is offered at the Alfred University School of Theology.

With the exception of the observance of the sabbath, the Seventh-Day Baptists are alike in their doctrinal position with all other Baptist groups in North America. They believe in the right of religious liberty and liberty of conscience, in the Bible as the final authority in matters of faith and conduct, in the separation of church and state, in believer's baptism by immersion, and they believe in salvation by faith in the Lord Jesus Christ. In their *Guide to Church Membership,* they state: "Our beliefs should be very precious to us. Particularly should this be true of our belief in the sabbath, for it is this belief which distinguishes us from most other Christians. Not that there is value in just being different, but this is one reason for our existence as a denomination—that we are Christian observers of the sabbath."

Southern Baptist Convention

The purpose of the Southern Baptist Convention, as stated in its constitution, is "to provide a general organization for Baptists in the United States and its territories for the promotion of Christian missions at home and abroad, and any other objects such as Christian education, benevolent enterprises, and social services which it may deem proper and advisable for the furtherance of the kingdom of God."

Technically, the Convention is made up of messengers from Baptist churches who are in "friendly co-operation with this Convention and sympathetic with its purposes and work and have during the fiscal year preceding been bona fide contributors to the Convention's work"; but the Southern Baptist Convention, as the term is generally used, is more than a group of messengers meeting a technical requirement. It represents: (1) a common theological point of view without the imposition of a rigid creedal statement; (2) an accepted pattern of work without the cold hand of absolute conformity; (3) a burning missionary passion, responding to voluntary life commitment and dedicated stewardship.

The Southern Baptist Convention was a different type of organization from the old Triennial Convention in that the various boards and agencies were responsible to the Convention itself, not independent societies. Within the past few years the Convention has written into its bylaws the provision that "the charters of all agencies shall provide that the trustees or directors of such agencies be elected by the Convention, and that their charters may not be further amended without the prior consent of the Convention." In 1956 the Convention included in its bylaws an action it had previously taken to the effect that "the Executive Committee shall not recommend any percentage allocation of funds for any agency or institution for which the Convention does not elect trustees or directors."

The Convention serves Southern Baptist churches through four general boards: Foreign Mission Board (1845); Home Mission Board (1845); Sunday School Board (1891); and Annuity Board (1918). The institutions operated and controlled by the Convention are: Golden Gate Seminary (1951); New Orleans Seminary (1917); Southeastern Seminary (1951); Southern Seminary (1859); Southwestern Seminary (1908); Midwestern Seminary (1957); Southern Baptist Foundation (1946); and Southern Baptist Hospitals: New Orleans, Louisiana (1926), Jacksonville, Florida (1955).

The commissions are: Baptist Brotherhood Commission

(1907); Education Commission (1916); Radio and Television Commission (1946); Christian Life Commission (1913); Historical Commission (1951); Commission on American Seminary (1924); and Stewardship Commission (1960).

The Committee on Public Affairs was established by the Convention in 1936.

The Foreign Mission Board reported 1,752 missionaries working in fifty-two mission areas in 1963. There were 187 emeritus missionaries. Southern Baptists have appointed a total of 2,947 missionaries since the organization of the Foreign Mission Board.

At the close of 1962 the Home Mission Board reported 2,078 missionaries, and 595 student workers were appointed for the summer of 1962, including those sponsored by Baptist Student Unions. The missionaries work among language groups, in rescue missions, in Cuba, in Panama and the Canal Zone, in Alaska, in the development of pioneer missions, and in joint development of mission programs with state mission boards. The Home Mission Board also has responsibility for the Division of Evangelism, for Jewish work, for work with the chaplains, and for the administration of church loan funds.

The Sunday School Board does not receive funds through the Cooperative Program but is responsible to the Convention for its operation. It is charged with the responsibility for the publication of literature and books, for the discovery and development of education and service for use in the churches, and for the operation of the Baptist Book Stores and the summer assemblies at Ridgecrest, North Carolina, and Glorieta, New Mexico. The Sunday School Board reported 1,259 employees, of whom 715 work in Nashville; the others work in Baptist Book Stores in other cities and at the two assemblies.

By action of the 1960 session of the Southern Baptist Convention, the Relief and Annuity Board became the Annuity

Board. It receives funds through the Cooperative Program only for the relief of and aid to retired ministers and their widows. The Cooperative Program makes $250,000 a year available for this needed ministry. The Annuity Board also administers the various pension plans for pastors and denominational employees.

The Executive Committee acts for the Convention ad interim "in all matters not otherwise provided for." It is "the executive agency of the Convention in all of its affairs not specifically committed to some other board or agency."

The Executive Committee has the responsibility for arranging the meetings of the Convention, acting in an advisory capacity in questions of co-operation between the different agencies of the Convention, presenting to the Convention each year a consolidated financial statement of all agencies, and recommending to the Convention a budget for the Convention and all its agencies.

The Executive Committee is also charged with the responsibility of conducting the general work of publicity and promotion for the Convention, in co-operation with the other agencies and institutions. It has no authority to control or direct the boards of the Convention, but it is instructed to study the affairs of the various agencies and to make such recommendations to them, or to the Convention concerning them, as it deems advisable.

The Southern Baptist Convention believes in co-operation. It co-operates with the American Bible Society, with various temperance organizations, and with groups in special programs; but it is not a member of either the National Council of Churches or the World Council of Churches.

The decision not to join these organizations has been based on (1) the concept that the Convention cannot take an action which would commit an individual congregation and (2) a feeling on the part of a great majority of Southern Baptists that the leaders of this movement are working toward church union, through the process of finding a common denominator of broad generalizations to replace positive convictions regarding the teachings of the Bible.

There are twenty-eight state conventions carrying on many programs in education, benevolence, and missions. There are 1,162 associations, involved largely in mission programs.

4

Laymen Have Helped

In a statement entitled *Baptist Ideals* prepared by the Baptist Jubilee Advance Committee of the Southern Baptist Convention, the section on the priesthood of the believer reads: "Every man is competent to go directly to God for forgiveness through repentance and faith. He needs neither individual nor church to dispense salvation. There is but one mediator of God and man, Jesus Christ our Lord. After one has become a Christian he has direct access to God through Christ. He has entered into a royal priesthood and is privileged to minister for Christ to all men. He is to share with them the faith he cherishes and to serve them in the name and spirit of his Lord. The priesthood of believers, therefore, means that all members serve as equals under God in the fellowship of a local church."

Historically, Baptist ministers have taken the leadership in the organization of the association, the state convention, and a national convention or federation, but a number of laymen have given sacrificially of their time and their experience to serve their Lord and their denomination. Most of these faithful laymen, who contribute significantly to the life of their church as Sunday school teachers, deacons, trustees, and in other capacities are given little public notice. Many have won wide recognition for their achievements in the fields of business, government, the professions, or in the life of their denomination.

The sketches which follow do not propose to be representative of all of the 77,000 churches, nor do they include hundreds who have won distinction. These represent only a cross section of many who could be named for their devotion to God in their full stewardship. Some of the sketches previously appeared in the author's booklet on the presidents of the Southern Baptist Convention.

Annie Armstrong

When thirty-two delegates from twelve states met to consider the organization of the Woman's Missionary Union, on May 11, 1888, in the basement of the Broad Street Methodist Church of Richmond, Virginia, there were some who voiced a word of caution, but Miss Annie Armstrong advocated immediate action without further delay.

When the Woman's Missionary Union was organized that year, Annie Armstrong was elected as the corresponding secretary and served in that position until 1906.

Annie Walker Armstrong was born in Baltimore on July 11, 1850. She did not become a Christian until she was nineteen years of age, when she was baptized into the membership of the Seventh Baptist Church by Richard Fuller. When the Eutaw Place Baptist Church was organized as a mission and as a church from the Seventh Baptist Church, she joined with 117 others in membership and taught the children's class there for thirty years.

During the years Miss Armstrong served as secretary for the Woman's Missionary Union, she would not receive any salary, and in 1888 she personally wrote by hand, letters to all of the societies asking them to contribute to the first Christmas offering which had been suggested by the now-famous Lottie Moon in China.

"Miss Annie," as she was known by women all over the Southern Baptist Convention, insisted that the Woman's Missionary Union should be auxiliary to the Southern Baptist Convention and should never attempt to carry on mission programs of its own. She felt that the WMU should promote and teach missions but should not serve as an agency of collection and administration in missions. She was also very active in work among Negro Baptist women. The Woman's Missionary Union has honored her memory by the Annie Armstrong Offering for Home Missions. Miss Armstrong died in Baltimore on December 20, 1938.

William Colgate

William Colgate was born January 25, 1783, in the County of Kent in England. His father was a fierce champion of religious liberty, and because of his beliefs and his sympathy with the colonies during the time of revolution, he was forced to flee England and came to the young United States. After several years of school in Baltimore, young William withdrew at the age of seventeen to engage in the soap and candle business. After a year he moved to New York to learn more about the business, and at twenty-three he started into business again for himself in New York City.

The Colgate home became a center for ministers to gather, and missionaries who were arriving in New York or leaving from New York were always invited.

In the Baptist Tabernacle where he attended, the story was told of the conversion of a woman of bad reputation. A question arose as to whether or not she should be accepted into the church. Deacon Colgate arose and said: "I think, brethren, we have been a little careless, and hereafter perhaps it would be wise for us to be more specific in our prayers. We have been praying for the conversion of sinners. But we have not told him what kind of sinners we desired him to save. He has saved, as we hoped, this sinful woman, and we don't know what to do—whether to receive her or not. Perhaps if we should be a little more careful hereafter to tell the Lord just what kind of sinners to convert, we may not have to be troubled."

William Colgate was one of the early leaders of the Sunday school movement in the United States, and took a leading part in the abolishment of pew rents as a method of church finance.

Baptists are faced with the problem of urbanization today, but Mr. Colgate saw the problem early as indicated by a resolution he introduced in the Hudson River Association in 1856. Faced with the growing population of New York and the decline in church attendance, Deacon Colgate proposed the following questions:

1. Can any change be made in the mode of conducting our religious services on the Lord's Day which will add to the interest and prosperity of our churches?

2. What can be done most effectually to reach and thoroughly cultivate the entire field within the boundaries of the several churches and of the Association, and would it be advisable to establish missionary stations or preaching in the open air; and if so, how can they best be sustained in the present embarrassed condition of many of our churches?

3. Would not a uniform rule as to Sunday collections have a tendency to strengthen our feeble churches by removing a distinction, which is sometimes felt to be odious, between them and more wealthy churches?

4. Can any means be suggested to awaken and increase a desire for more frequent conversation upon religious subjects in the families and social intercourse of Christian men and women?

5. Can any improvement be made in the mode of conducting Sunday schools, and in the selection of books for their libraries?

6. Can any way be devised to correct the growing habit of attending church to gratify or improve the intellect as the chief object, rather than to worship God?

7. Can any improvement be made in the ordinary mode of conducting family devotion, so as more effectually to interest all alike in the discharge of this important duty?

8. Can any change be made in conducting our meetings for social prayer and conference, so as to increase their usefulness?

9. What few books, easily obtainable, can be selected which can be recommended as best adapted to awaken the unconverted and promote domestic piety?

William Fleming

On May 5, 1963, a sudden heart attack brought death to William Fleming, whose benefactions have brought financial assistance to Baptist churches and institutions around the world, and whose Christian compassion had brought Christ to many men whose lives he touched in the oil business.

William Fleming grew up in Fannin County, Texas, and spent his early years in Whitewright. In assessing the factors which led to his zealous Christian spirit, Mr. Fleming often recalled one experience of those early years.

"When a young man and a resident of Whitewright, I had an attack of appendicitis. The appendix ruptured. My body was swollen nearly the size of two bodies. Gangrene set in and the doctors instructed the nurse to keep me comfortable until the end.

"A neighbor came to see how I was doing. He was Jim Truett, brother to Dr. George Truett, and when he saw my condition he went to another room to pray. After an hour of agonizing prayer, he emerged to say, 'This man will not die. I have an answer from the Lord.'"

With a firm belief that the Lord had spared his life, William Fleming had great faith in prayer. During his early business experience he went to the bank and borrowed $15,000 to help his church through a crisis, as an answer to prayer and with assurance that it was God's will. He would show how the fortunes changed by reporting the same year he sold a part of his oil holdings for over one million dollars.

Mr. Fleming was chairman of the trustees of Southwestern Seminary and also served as the chairman and a member of the Texas Baptist Foundation for many years. He was president of the Texas Baptist Convention for two years and led the state in a new surge of evangelistic interest. It was said of him that no man who came into his office to discuss oil business or real estate business would leave until Mr. Fleming had first found out about his spiritual condition.

Mr. and Mrs. Fleming were especially interested in the opportunities in the West and made several significant contributions to Grand Canyon Baptist College and to churches in Colorado, Oregon, Washington, and western Canada.

Mr. Fleming recounted many times his experience when his first oil well came in. As the oil started spraying over the rig, Mr. Fleming entered the tool house and got down on his knees in the oil for a moment of prayer. "It looks like I am a wealthy man, Lord; please don't let it make a fool of me." The Lord answered that prayer.

Jonathan Haralson

When the thirty-fourth session of the Southern Baptist Convention was called to order on May 10, 1889, in the First Baptist Church, Memphis, Tennessee, the president's chair was empty. President James P. Boyce had died during the year, and there was some confusion when Lewis Bell Ely of Carrollton, Missouri, took the gavel and called for the organization of the Convention.

In those early days the election of officers was one of the first items of business. When the nominations were opened, Dr. M. B. Wharton of Montgomery, Alabama, a man of wide experience and acquaintance in the South, nominated a layman he had come to know and love in Alabama, Judge Jonathan Haralson. When the votes were counted, Judge Haralson, who had been elected as a vice-president in 1887, was the new president, the first layman to hold that office in the history of the Convention.

Jonathan Haralson was born in Lowndes County, Alabama,

October 18, 1830. He attended the University of Alabama while Dr. Basil Manly was serving as president and then went on to Louisiana, where he completed his work in a law school in New Orleans in 1852. He settled in Selma in 1853, just at the time Baptist work was being firmly established there. His first pastor was Rev. A. G. McCraw, a man with a vision reaching to the ends of the earth. Other pastors who served during the period Jonathan Haralson lived at Selma were the eloquent J. B. Hawthorne and the tireless J. M. Frost, who later was to take the lead in the organization of the present Sunday School Board.

Judge Haralson went to Europe on several legal cases, served with distinction in the lower courts of Alabama, and climaxed his legal service as an associate justice of the Supreme Court of Alabama from 1892 until 1910.

He applied the same industry to the activities of his church and denomination that he did to his legal career. In 1874 he was elected as president of the Alabama Baptist State Convention, and he served with distinction until 1889 when he was elected as president of the Southern Baptist Convention, a position he held for ten years.

After Judge Haralson's death at Montgomery in July, 1912, Dr. J. M. Frost wrote, "I have seen mighty men as presiding officers, but to my thinking and yet without disparagement to others, I never saw his superior in wielding the gavel and directing the forces of a great assembly. He was equally great whether the Convention was in a mighty storm, as sometimes happened in those days, or was under the influence of a great surging wave of spiritual influence."

James Franklin Jarman

Around the world, Baptists will find church buildings in many countries built or assisted in building by the Jarman Foundation, which was started by James Franklin Jarman, chairman of the board of the General Shoe Corporation and leading Baptist layman, and carried on by his son, Maxey Jarman, now chairman of the board of Genesco.

James Franklin Jarman was born in Murfreesboro, Tennessee, on July 28, 1867, one of eight children. When he was a child, the Jarman family moved to Jackson, Tennessee, where the father served several years as president of Union University, and James Franklin was graduated with a Master of Arts degree in 1884.

As a young man, Frank Jarman went into the shoe business, first as a salesman and then as a manufacturer, finally founding as a partner the J. W. Carter Shoe Company in 1902. He told many times of his Christian experience and of how he was a nominal Christian until attending a revival service in Cleveland, Ohio, where he heard Dr. R. A. Torrey preach. Dr. Torrey took as his text, "Where Art Thou?" and somehow this penetrated the heart of Mr. Jarman. About midnight that night he came to see himself as an undeserving sinner and surrendered his life completely to the lordship of Jesus Christ. He resigned his office as Sunday school superintendent and as deacon and insisted he be rebaptized. Again, he was elected as a deacon and as Sunday school superintendent.

For many years Mr. Jarman served as a member of the Sunday School Board of the Southern Baptist Convention. He also took an active interest in the Tennessee Baptist orphanages and was a trustee of Peabody College. He was active many years as a deacon in the First Baptist Church and was the superintendent of the Sunday school. He died on August 23, 1938. The Jarman Shoe Company and the "Friendly Five" shoes grew even during the depression years.

The Genesco Corporation, carried on by his son, Maxey Jarman, is now one of the nation's leading manufacturers and distributors not only of shoes but of all types of clothing and wearing apparel.

Joshua Levering

One of the great Baptist laymen of the past century was Eugene Levering, Sr., of Baltimore, Maryland. With his brother, he built one of the largest coffee importing and shipping concerns in the United States.

Eugene Levering, Sr., not only developed a great business, but he also developed a Christian home. Among his twelve children were twins, Eugene, Jr., and Joshua, born on September 12, 1845. Richard Fuller, one of the leading Baptist ministers of his day, was a frequent visitor in the home and guided demonstrated in one incident in the life of the father. Much the family in making Christ the center of all life.

An example of their Christian attitude in all areas of life is of the firm's business was in the South. When the War Between the States broke out in 1861, the business was forced to settle more than $100,000 in debts for half of the value. When good business returned after the war, the firm redeemed all debts in full, although there was no legal obligation.

The sons continued to build the business, and both of them continued their interest in Christian activities.

One of the early leaders in the Prohibition movement in the United States, Joshua Levering was the Prohibition candidate for President of the United States in 1896. For many years he was the president of the board of trustees of the Southern Baptist Theological Seminary in Louisville. His gifts made possible the building of the Levering Gymnasium on the seminary campus. He also served as a member of the Foreign Mission Board, and it is reported that the Bagbys, first Southern Baptist missionaries to Brazil, went out on a Levering ship.

In 1908 Joshua Levering became president of the Southern Baptist Convention and served through 1910.

He died in Baltimore on October 5, 1935, at the age of ninety-one.

Pat M. Neff

Three men who have served as president of the Southern Baptist Convention have also served as governor of the states in which they lived. The first was W. J. Northen of Georgia. The second was James P. Eagle of Arkansas. Pat Morris Neff of Texas was the third.

When the Southern Baptist Convention met in San Antonio, Texas, in May, 1942, the feeling was expressed by many messengers that it was time for a layman to serve as president again. It had been more than thirty years since Joshua Levering, another great Christian layman, had served. Pat Neff was unanimously elected.

Pat Morris Neff was born at McGregor, Texas, November 26, 1871. He received his Bachelor of Arts degree from Baylor University in 1894 and then went on to the University of Texas, where he received his law degree in 1897. He then returned to Baylor where he received his master's degree in 1898.

After graduation he opened his practice of law in Waco and gained distinction as a legislator and as a prosecuting attorney. In 1921 he was elected governor of Texas and served for two terms. From 1927 to 1929 he served as a member of the United States Board of Mediation, and then for two years he was chairman of the Texas Railroad Commission.

For more than a quarter of a century he served as president of the board of trustees of Baylor University. It is significant that the trustees, in 1932, turned to him as president to succeed Dr. Brooks, who had died during the year. Pat Neff served as president of Baylor until 1947, when he retired.

Serving as president was no new experience, for Pat Neff had served as president of the Texas Baptist Convention, and in 1933 had been elected vice-president of the Southern Baptist Convention. He encouraged the messengers to feel that discussion was open to all, and the number of messengers participating in the discussions greatly increased during his tenure.

Pat Neff believed in Baptists—and, above all, he believed in God. In 1943, when the Convention had to be deferred because of the war, he wrote, "Let us all with courage and undiminishing zeal go on with the work which has been committed to us. While we walk in the midst of tribulation and the shadows of destruction lengthen upon the earth, we yet can trust in him who created man in his own image; we can depend upon him to lead us out of the darkness; we can 'sail ahead, and leave the rest to God.'"

Dr. Neff died in Waco, Texas, on January 20, 1952.

John D. Rockefeller, Sr. and Jr.

Any list of Baptist laymen who have achieved success in the business realm and have at the same time maintained a serious interest in their own spiritual development and the spiritual development of the world would include the names of John D. Rockefeller, Sr. and John D. Rockefeller, Jr.

John D. Rockefeller, Sr. attended the Sunday school and church at the First Baptist Church in Oswego, New York, before moving to Cleveland. When he was fourteen years of age, the family started attending the Erie Street Baptist Church (which later became the Euclid Avenue Church), and at the age of fifteen young Rockefeller made a profession of faith and was baptized. He found a great deal of interest in his church and was made the clerk of the church and conducted a Sunday school class soon after his baptism. The church was the center of his social activity as well as his way of life, and he believed that tithing, attendance at the church services, Sunday school, and prayer meeting were but minimums in his religious life.

The family custom in the Rockefeller, Sr. home called for family prayers before breakfast, with each one taking part either through reading the Scriptures or through reciting a verse. On Sunday evening Mrs. Rockefeller would gather the children for a "home talk" and out of these family experiences grew the conversion and baptism of John D., Jr. when he was nearly ten years of age.

When John D., Jr. was still a teen-ager, the family moved to New York and the church there continued to be the center of interest in their lives. The younger Rockefeller was influenced by W. H. P. Faunce, his young pastor, to enrol in Brown University, a Baptist school. While in Brown, he volunteered as a teacher of a boys' Bible class at the Central Baptist Church of Providence and took part in YMCA activities.

During the early years of the 1900's the father and son together set up the Rockefeller Institute for Medical Research, the General Education Board, and the Rockefeller Foundation. Through these funds and other channels, the Rockefellers contributed, including income and principal, nearly a billion dollars for various religious, educational, research, and benevolent programs. It was during this same period that the Rockefellers were attacked for manipulations in the petroleum business.

With the coming of World War I, John D. Rockefeller, Jr. was disillusioned regarding social progress, and felt very strongly that the church in its structure had failed to meet the challenge of the hour. He became a strong supporter of the Inter-Church World Movement, and although this failed, he continued to be until his death a strong supporter of various ecumenical programs. He withdrew his support from the American Baptist Foreign Mission Society but continued to give through his church.

E. W. Stephens

Edwin William Stephens, the ninth president of the Southern Baptist Convention, served as president of thirty-five different boards, commissions, conventions, and associations during his life. He was moderator of his association, moderator of the Missouri Baptist Association, vice-president of the Northern Baptist Convention, president of the Southern Baptist Convention, president of the short-lived Baptist General Convention of America, and American treasurer of the Baptist World Alliance.

In secular life, E. W. was editor and publisher of the Columbia *Herald* for thirty-five years, president of the E. W. Stephens Publishing Company, of the National Editorial Association, and of the YMCA of Missouri.

Edwin William Stephens was born in Columbia, Missouri, January 21, 1849. His father, James L. Stephens, had come to Missouri from Kentucky in 1819 and had soon established a thriving business. His contributions made possible the early work of Stephens College.

James L. Stephens had played a big part in the location of the University of Missouri at Columbia. E. W. inherited his father's interest in the University of Missouri and was also very much interested in William Jewell College. He had much to do with the founding of the famous School of Journalism at the University of Missouri.

After his unanimous election as president of the Southern Baptist Convention in 1905, Mr. Stephens made a world tour. He represented Southern Baptists at the meeting of the Baptist World Alliance, and his speech before twelve thousand people in the great Albert Hall in London demonstrated his grasp of Baptist opportunities in the world. President Stephens made an excellent presiding officer, and as one writer phrased it, "He knew just when to yield the rigid letter of parliamentary law in the interest of good humor that occasionally seeks demonstration in a great religious body."

Although Mr. Stephens had a vision of the world opportunities which Baptists faced, he never lost interest in the work of his own church, the First Baptist of Columbia, Missouri. In

addition to other activities, he taught a Sunday School class
there for thirty-one years.

A lifelong resident of Columbia, Mr. Stephens died there on
May 22, 1931, at the age of eighty-three.

Booker T. Washington

At about the time of President Buchanan's inauguration
speech and the Supreme Court decision in the Dred Scott
Case, which started anew those forces which eventually led to
the War Between the States, a Negro slave boy was born near
a crossroads post office called Hale's Ford, in Franklin County,
Virginia. The exact date of his birth is not known but it was
assumed from other occurrences that it was about 1857.

With the coming of the surrender of the Confederate armies,
Booker T. Washington's family moved to West Virginia where
his stepfather had gone to work in the salt mines. When the
time came to enrol in school, the boy had to have a last name.
Having read of George Washington, he selected this as his
last name and later inserted the middle name Taliaferro. In his
school he learned of Hampton Institute in Virginia where a
young man could go if he had the will, and young Booker had
the will, which finally led to his graduation from Wayland
Seminary in Washington and then to the presidency of Tuske-
gee Institute in 1881.

For his service in Negro education, Booker T. Washington
was honored by his state, by his nation, and by various educational institutions, including an honorary degree from Harvard
University. He appeared before Congress to make a plea for
an appropriation to assist in the Atlanta exposition in 1905,
and his speech at that exposition was acclaimed by national
leaders both white and Negro as setting a course for years to
come. He said, "To those of my race who depend on bettering
their condition in a foreign land or who underestimate the importance of cultivating friendly relations with the Southern

white man, who is their next-door neighbour, I would say: 'Cast down your bucket where you are'—cast it down in making friends in every manly way of the people of all races by whom we are surrounded."

Booker T. Washington concluded his speech, which has meaning even in our day, by stating, "I pledge that in your effort to work out the great and intricate problem which God has laid at the doors of the South, you shall have at all times the patient, sympathetic help of my race; only let this be constantly in mind, that, while from representations in these buildings of the product of field, of forest, of mine, of factory, letters, and art, much good will come, yet far above and beyond material benefits will be that higher good, that, let us pray God, will come, in a blotting out of sectional differences and racial animosities and suspicions, in a determination to administer absolute justice, in a willing obedience among all classes to the mandates of law. This, this, coupled with our material prosperity, will bring into our beloved South a new heaven and a new earth."

Booker T. Washington was one of the outstanding Baptist laymen of his day. He delivered an address at the National Baptist Convention at Chicago just a month before his death on November 14, 1915.

5

They Came Preaching

A common characteristic of the development of the 77,000 Baptist churches in the seven Baptist groups participating in the Baptist Jubilee Advance has been the centrality of their preaching ministry.

In the days when the Triennial Convention was first organized, preaching and music constituted most of the church service. It has only been in the past fifty years that major attention has been given to Bible teaching and training, and more recently to counseling in practically all Baptist churches.

The men who preach from the pulpits of Baptist churches in North America are diverse in their training and method. In the early days of the Triennial Convention, many of the leading pastors had no formal education, although many of them had been ardent students. Thomas Baldwin, pastor in Boston, and Richard Fuller, the first president of the Triennial Convention, had no formal theological education. Both had utilized books and personal tutors to assist them in their training. On the other hand, William Staughton of Philadelphia was a graduate of Bristol College in England, and Richard Fuller was a graduate of Harvard.

A growing percentage of Baptist pastors in North America are graduates of colleges and seminaries, but God is not limited in his use of a man without this type of training in some places of service.

The sketches presented of ministers who have served in

70

North America during these one hundred fifty years is not intended to be comprehensive but illustrative. Some of these sketches appeared in the author's booklet on the presidents of the Southern Baptist Convention. No living ministers are presented in these sketches.

James P. Boyce

About 1683 two groups of settlers arrived in South Carolina, near Charles Town. One group came from the west of England. The second group came from Kittery, in the state of Maine. Love of truth and persecution for belief was a common experience, and it was not long before they were joined in what was to become the First Baptist Church of Charleston, South Carolina.

This church was to produce many outstanding Baptist characters in the years ahead. One of the most illustrious of her sons was James Petigru Boyce, the fifth president of the Southern Baptist Convention. He was born in Charleston on January 11, 1827. His father was one of the financial leaders of the old South. Among the Sunday school teachers of young Boyce were Charles H. Lanneau, one of the great laymen of his day, and Henry Allen Tupper, who later became secretary of the Southern Baptist Foreign Mission Board.

While young Boyce was a student in Brown University, from which he was graduated in 1847, he accepted Christ and was baptized by the Rev. Richard Fuller in 1846. After completing his work at Brown, he felt the call to enter the ministry and entered the Princeton Theological Seminary. In 1851 he was ordained and called as pastor of the Baptist church at Columbia, South Carolina.

While teaching at Furman, James P. Boyce saw the need for a theological seminary for the Southern Baptist Convention. He poured his life and his wealth into the founding of the Southern Baptist Theological Seminary. He was the first chairman of the faculty and the first general agent. In the dark days following the Civil War, he was offered $10,000 a year, a fabulous salary for that time, to serve as president of a railroad. Even though the seminary could not pay his salary at the time, he replied, "Thank the gentleman for me, but tell them I must decline, as I have decided to devote my life, if need be, to building the Southern Baptist Theological Seminary."

Writing of Dr. Boyce as president of the Southern Baptist Convention, Dr. John A. Broadus said, "To preside well over a big Baptist convention is no ordinary task; the Speaker in the national House of Representatives . . . has scarcely greater difficulties to overcome. Every Baptist of them all feels himself perfectly free, and wishes to be personally uncontrolled, and yet all desire that the president shall maintain perfect order." Dr. Boyce met those qualifications.

Dr. Boyce went to France in 1888 for his health and died at Pau, in the south of France, on December 28, 1888.

Benajah Harvey Carroll

Church records at Caldwell, Texas, for 1865 show that in the regular conference in October, 1865, "the committee appointed to see Harvey Carroll for dancing reported that he requested to be excluded from the church. On motion the church withdrew fellowship from him." The next record of Benajah Harvey Carroll was in May, 1866, when he was licensed to preach, and then again in November, 1866, when he was ordained.

In between these two dates there was the conversion experience of B. H. Carroll who, although listed on the church roll, was an active infidel.

B. H. Carroll was born December 27, 1843, in Carroll County, Mississippi. At the age of seven the family moved to Arkansas and when he was fifteen the family moved to Caldwell in central Texas. Young Carroll attended Baylor University although he was never graduated. During the War Between the States, although he was against secession, he became a Texas Ranger and fought for the Confederacy.

Following the war, B. H. Carroll returned to Caldwell and became a schoolteacher and then after his ordination a farmer-preacher. He was called as pastor of the First Baptist Church of Waco in 1870 but would not leave his country church until 1871; this pastorate lasted for twenty-eight years.

Dr. Carroll's scholarship was a challenge to the students of Baylor University. It was only natural that the vision of Southwestern Seminary should grow in his mind as he presented it to the trustees of Baylor University and finally led in the movement to Fort Worth with Dr. Carroll as first president. It was said of Dr. Carroll that he read an average of three hundred pages a day for more than fifty years and could remember verbatim entire pages and even chapters.

At the meeting of the Southern Baptist Convention in 1905, one of the last he attended, one of the scheduled speakers did not appear and Dr. Carroll was asked to speak. His wide knowledge of history, of science, of the Bible, and of literature was so reflected in the organization and sweep of his message, that the audience stood to their feet and cheered when he concluded. This was unusual in the life of the Southern Baptist Convention. He died on Seminary Hill in Fort Worth on November 11, 1914.

Richard Fuller

First in his class at Harvard at the age of sixteen! An outstanding South Carolina attorney at the age of twenty-four! A prominent layman in the Episcopal church at the age of twenty-four! A Baptist preacher at the age of twenty-eight! The third president of the Southern Baptist Convention at the age of fifty-five!

If Richard Fuller were living today instead of in the last century, his decisions would be the subject for many newspaper feature stories. He was born at Beaufort, South Carolina, April 22, 1804. Young Richard entered Harvard with literary ambitions, but in his senior year he had a hemorrhage of the lungs and had to withdraw. He returned to Beaufort and turned his attention to the law. At the age of twenty-eight he was making more than $6,000 a year, a very large sum in that time. He was being mentioned for high political office in South Carolina.

In 1831 Richard Fuller had united with the Episcopal church. However, in the same year, he heard a great Baptist evangelist, Daniel Baker, and he realized that his days as a lawyer were ended. He was baptized into the fellowship of the Baptist church in Beaufort. The next year he was called as pastor at Beaufort and "resolved never to insult the Master with indolent preparation or superficial and ineffectual performance." It is reported that he baptized one hundred converts on the day he was ordained in 1832.

In 1847 Richard Fuller was called as pastor in Baltimore, where he remained until his death. He is listed as the preacher of the first Convention sermon, and his message on "The Cross," with the text taken from John 12:32, was preached with such power that he was asked to preach it at some time during each Convention until 1862. As he passed away on October 20, 1876, he murmured again and again, "Who'll preach Jesus?"

J. B. Gambrell

"More people, a hundred to one, will join in a bear hunt than will turn out to kill a mouse."

"A desire to get up in the ministry has kept many a man down in the ministry."

"A degree is like a promissory note. The value of it depends on what is back of it."

"I could never admire the dog with a noble voice that gave its nights to barking at crickets."

"Mud will rub off much easier when it is dry."

These are but a few of the quotations picked at random from the many sage observations of J. B. Gambrell. For "Uncle Gideon," as he was affectionately known by thousands of Southern Baptist ministers, had a pithy way of putting things that would clear the atmosphere and make right decisions easy. "As Dr. Gambrell used to say" is still a familiar phrase used by many Southern Baptist preachers.

James Bruton Gambrell was born in Anderson County, South Carolina, August 21, 1841. The family soon moved to Mississippi, and it is reported that the father missed only two services in twenty-five years as a faithful member of the old Pleasant Ridge Baptist Church in Mississippi.

During the War Between the States, young Gambrell enlisted in a company commanded by his teacher, Capt. R. M. Leavell, and he became a daring scout in the Confederate Army.

In 1866 he was licensed to preach by the Pleasant Ridge Church, and the next year the Cherry Creek Church ordained him. While attending the University of Mississippi, he served as pastor at Oxford. During his five years at Oxford, J. B. Gambrell gained such a wide reputation as a writer that he was elected editor of the Mississippi *Baptist Record* in 1877. Soon the attention of the entire South was focused on his editorials and followed them until 1893.

After a short term as president of Mercer University, Dr. Gambrell was elected mission secretary in Texas. Baptists there were facing difficult days in 1896 when Dr. Gambrell unpacked, but his ready wit and his Christian courage set the stage for progress. He was aided greatly by his gifted wife, who was elected secretary of the women's missionary work. He later served as editor of the *Baptist Standard* and as professor in Southwestern Seminary.

J. B. Gambrell was seventy-eight when elected president of the Southern Baptist Convention, but he was a man of great vigor. While he was president of the Convention women were first admitted as messengers, the Relief and Annuity Board was created, the Seventy-five Million Campaign was launched, and Baptists rejected the bid of the interchurch movement. Southern Baptists have never wavered from the stand Dr. Gambrell took at a tense moment in the Southern Baptist Convention when he declared, "Southern Baptists do not ride a horse without a bridle."

The great commoner among Southern Baptists died in Dallas, Texas, on June 10, 1921.

John Jasper

The most famous of the Negro Baptist preachers of the nineteenth century was John Jasper, the Richmond minister of the Sixth Mount Zion Church for more than fifty years.

John Jasper spent his boyhood as a slave on a Virginia plantation and moved to Richmond as a young man where he was sold to a tobacco manufacturer. He continued as a slave preacher for twenty-five years, and although uneducated, unable to read, and untutored as far as the fields of science are concerned, he had a tremendous influence in the city of Richmond. Although his sermons might have been heard by some for entertainment, he had a way of driving the truth of the gospel home.

Not much is known of John Jasper's birth, but he did know the reality of his conversion on July 25, 1839, and from that day until his death, at the age of eighty-nine, he was a flaming evangel.

His sermon on "The Sun Do Move," and his concept of a flat earth, caused many of his Negro co-workers to feel that he was degrading their race, but he touched the lives of many people and led in developing the life of his church. In his own personal habits and character, he was a living testimony to the grace of God.

William B. Johnson

George Washington, first president of the United States, went to Georgetown, South Carolina, in 1791 for a reception, and one of the admirers to shake his hand was a nine-year-old lad, William Bullein Johnson, who some fifty years later, in 1845, was to become the first president of the Southern Baptist Convention.

Dr. Johnson remembered with pleasure his meeting with George Washington, but it was a meeting with Luther Rice at the Savannah River Association in 1813 that was to have greater meaning in his life. When Luther Rice told of the experience he had shared with Adoniram Judson, W. B. Johnson caught a world vision he was never to lose.

The Savannah River Missionary Society, one of the first in the South, was organized immediately after Rice's visit, and Johnson became the first president. He suggested that the meeting place for representatives of other mission societies be Philadelphia, and when the Triennial Convention was organized in 1814, Dr. Johnson not only served on the committee to draft the constitution, but was also named as the corresponding secretary of its Foreign Mission Board.

As a young man, W. B. Johnson had studied law and had attended Brown University. This training was of real value as he not only assisted in preparing the constitution for the Triennial Convention, but also served on the committee preparing the constitution when the South Carolina convention was organized in 1821, and when the Southern Baptist Convention was organized in Augusta, Georgia, in 1845.

As president of the Triennial Convention from 1841 to 1845, Dr. Johnson did much to try to iron out the differences between the North and the South, but finally he came to the conclusion that greater good could be accomplished through two conventions. He told the Savannah River Association shortly after the Augusta Convention, "Our objects then are the extension of the Messiah's kingdom, and the glory of our God. Not disunion with any of his people; not the upholding of any form of human policy, or civil rights; but God's glory, and Messiah's increasing reign."

Dr. Johnson's crowning work was the part he played in the organization of the Southern Baptist Theological Seminary, and he had the pleasure of being present in Greenville for the opening session in 1859 to offer the dedicatory prayer.

William Bullein Johnson died in Greenville, South Carolina, on October 2, 1862. He had dedicated his life to the uniting of Southern Baptists for the projection of the great missionary fire that burned in his heart. He had given a son as one of the first of Southern Baptists' missionaries to China.

E. Y. Mullins

On January 5, 1860, a young pastor of a country Baptist church in Franklin County, Mississippi, knelt by the crib of his first-born son and prayed earnestly that some day God might call the boy to be a minister of the gospel.

The child was given the name Edgar Young Mullins. He not only became a minister, but lived to serve as president of the Southern Baptist Theological Seminary, of the Southern Baptist Convention, and of the Baptist World Alliance.

In 1868 the Mullins family moved to Corsicana, Texas. As there were eleven children in the family, young Edgar found employment as a messenger boy and later as a telegrapher to help meet expenses. He even helped his older sisters to attend Baylor.

Young Mullins planned to study law—not to preach; at the time of his graduation from Texas A. & M. he had not even accepted Christ as his Saviour. He was working in Dallas as an expert telegrapher for the Associated Press when, on October 30, 1880, he went with a friend to hear Maj. W. E. Penn, the evangelist. God touched his heart, and that night he became a Christian.

When Edgar Young Mullins accepted Christ, he surrendered all of life. He entered the seminary at Louisville in 1881 and received his degree for the full course in 1885. A few weeks after graduation, on June 6, he was ordained by the First Baptist Church at Harrodsburg, Kentucky, to which he had been called as pastor. A year later he married Isla May Hawley. The young couple had a desire to go to Brazil as missionaries, but the financial condition of the Foreign Mission Board closed that door. Later, in 1896, Dr. Mullins did serve for a brief period as associate secretary of the Foreign Mission Board.

On June 29, 1899, Dr. Mullins was called to lead the Southern Baptist Theological Seminary as president during a period of crisis in the history of the school. He accepted the responsibility and served with great distinction until his death on November 23, 1928. He led in the building of the new seminary campus; and great scholar that he was, he made a tremendous contribution to Baptist life, particularly through his books: *The Axioms of Religion, Baptist Beliefs,* and *The Christian Religion in Its Doctrinal Expression.*

Dr. W. O. Carver wrote in tribute to Dr. Mullins at the time of his death: "Dr. Mullins stands in the minds of those who knew him best as an intelligent, determined, conquering instrument of the redemptive will of God. He led by following Jesus Christ."

Elias Camp Morris

A trained cobbler like William Carey, Elias Camp Morris was the leader of Negro Baptists in the early days of their organization, and piloted their convention through perilous waters and times of tension.

E. C. Morris was born in Murray County, Georgia, of slave parents in May, 1855. When the slaves were freed, the parents moved to Chattanooga, Tennessee, and later to Stephenson, Alabama, where young Elias finished his elementary school work and served an apprenticeship in shoemaking.

At nineteen years of age, Elias Camp Morris was converted and baptized in the Morning Star Baptist Church in Stephenson and the next year he was licensed and ordained to preach. After two years in Stephenson, he moved to Helena, Arkansas, where he again became a shoemaker and soon was called as pastor of the church.

The young Negro pastor was elected secretary of the Arkansas Baptist State Convention in 1880 and in 1882 was elected president. He was also named as a state missionary under the American Baptist Home Mission Society. He became president of the National Baptist Convention after its merger with the Foreign Mission Convention in 1895 and served for twenty-eight years.

John R. Sampey

"As I lay on the trundle bed on the night of March 3, 1877, I could not go to sleep. We had just had family prayers, and Father was reading and Mother was knitting. My younger brother had fallen asleep beside me; but I was in distress over my sins. In my desperation I lifted my eyes upward and began to talk in a whisper to the Saviour. I said to him: 'Lord Jesus, I do not know what to do. I have prayed, but I get no relief. I have read the Bible, but my sins are still a burden on my soul. I have listened to preaching, but find no help. I do not know what to do except to turn it all over to you; and if I am lost, I will go down trusting you.'"

John Richard Sampey never got away from his conversion experience. He told it, with tears of joy running down his cheeks, on hundreds of occasions. He repeated it in his memoirs. It became the dynamic for a great life dedicated to preaching and teaching.

John Richard Sampey was born at Fort Deposit, Alabama, September 27, 1863. His father had been a Methodist preacher, but as he read his Bible he had become convinced that the Baptist position was more in accord with New Testament teachings. He had joined a Baptist church and had been ordained as a Baptist minister.

Young John was licensed to preach when he was fifteen. He was graduated from Howard College with highest honors at the age of twenty-one. He completed his graduate course at Southern Seminary in 1885.

Dr. Sampey remained at the Louisville seminary as teacher and president for more than half a century. During his tenure as teacher, he taught Hebrew and Old Testament to more students than had any other teacher. Because of his ability to make the characters of the Old Testament live, he was given the name "Tiglath-pileser" by his students. He was known affectionately as "Old Tig." He was especially effective in making the students see the character of the founder of the second Assyrian empire.

When Dr. E. Y. Mullins died in November, 1928, Dr. Sampey was named as the acting president of Southern Seminary; he was named president in May, 1929. He served in this capacity until he retired from active duty in 1942. He also served as a pastor of churches near Louisville. He made a real contribution to the Christian life in South America and China through his evangelistic tours. He succeeded the late Dr. Broadus as a member of the International Uniform Sunday School Lesson Committee, serving for forty-six years in that work. He was president of the Southern Baptist Convention from 1936 to 1938.

Dr. Sampey passed away Sunday afternoon, August 8, 1946, in Louisville.

L. R. *Scarborough*

Lee Rutland Scarborough was born in Colfax, Louisiana, July 4, 1870. When he was four years of age, the family moved to Texas.

When Lee was graduated from Baylor University, his parents and many of his friends prayed that he would go on to the seminary and train for the ministry. But the young man was interested in law, and he went to Yale to take graduate work in law. However, before the end of the first year he wrote to his mother, "I have surrendered to preach. Please show this letter to my father."

In 1899 Lee Scarborough attended the Southern Baptist Theological Seminary, but the death of his brother brought his formal education to an end.

In 1908 Dr. B. H. Carroll persuaded Dr. Scarborough to leave a successful pastorate at Abilene, Texas, to build a "chair of fire"—evangelism—at Southwestern Seminary. Succeeding Dr. Carroll as president in 1916, he served in that capacity until he retired in 1942. Following Dr. Scarborough's example, hundreds of young men have gone out to "preach the Word" with evangelistic fervor.

As director of the Seventy-five Million Campaign, Dr. Scarborough literally gave his very heart and life to Southern Baptists and to the cause of Christ around the world. In addition to serving as president of the Texas Baptist Convention and of the Southern Baptist Convention, he was elected vice-president of the Baptist World Alliance in 1940.

Dr. Scarborough died in April, 1945.

At the dedication of beautiful Scarborough Hall at Southwestern Seminary on February 8, 1950, Dr. C. E. Matthews said: "Simplicity of speech, sincerity of purpose, and human approach to man were the three great qualities of Dr. Scarborough. . . . He was a natural leader of men, standing out

in any crowd. He knew no fear save the fear of God." In closing, Dr. Matthews said that Dr. Scarborough is "now living in
two worlds—in this one through his influence and in the other
in person." Appropriately enough, the memento which Mrs.
Scarborough chose to place in the cornerstone was a copy of
With Christ After the Lost, a text used by Dr. Scarborough
when he taught the course in evangelism at Southwestern
Seminary.

William Staughton

The first corresponding secretary of the American Baptist
Board of Foreign Missions was William Staughton of Philadelphia. He was born January 4, 1770, in Coventry, England.
At the age of seventeen he had a glorious conversion experience and entered Bristol College to study for the ministry.

At the time of his graduation in 1793, William Staughton was
called to the church at Northampton where Dr. Ryland had
been the pastor, but at the same time Dr. Rippon in Bristol
received a letter from Richard Furman inquiring about a man
to go to Georgetown, South Carolina. Dr. Rippon wrote that
William Staughton was the man, and so he sailed for the new
United States.

During the eighteen months he stayed at Georgetown, he
was married to Maria Hanson by Dr. Furman, then he went to
Bordentown, New Jersey, where he was principal of the school
and pastor of the church. He accepted the pastorate of the
First Baptist Church in Philadelphia in 1805 and stayed there
until 1811, when he went to the Sansom Street church in Philadelphia.

William Staughton took a leading part in the organization
of the Triennial Convention and later became president of
Columbian College in Washington. In 1829 he was elected
president of Georgetown College in Kentucky but died on his
way to his new post.

George W. Truett

Shortly before the death of Dr. George W. Truett on July 8, 1944, a friend visited the famous preacher. Aware of Dr. Truett's inability to sleep because of his intense suffering, the friend asked if the nights did not seem long.

"No!" Dr. Truett replied firmly. "I start counting the good things God has done for me, and the kindnesses of many friends, and the nights are not long enough."

At the time of Dr. Truett's death the secret of his preaching was said to be this: Like many other preachers, Dr. Truett spent many hours preparing his sermon—but he spent many more hours preparing himself in prayer.

This man has been called the greatest preacher produced by Southern Baptists.

George Washington Truett was born in a humble home on May 6, 1867, in Clay County, North Carolina. At the age of nineteen, he was converted in a rural revival while teaching at the Crooked Creek School. A short time after his conversion, the family moved to Texas.

Ordained as a minister by the Whitewright church in 1890, he soon won a wide reputation as a preacher. Soon Texas Baptists asked him to lead in a campaign to free Baylor University from debt. When the campaign was completed in 1893, Mr. Truett entered Baylor as a freshman. He served as pastor in Waco while he was in school. In 1894 he married Josephine Jenkins.

When George W. Truett was graduated from Baylor in 1897, he was called to the pastorate of the First Baptist Church in Dallas, where he remained until his death in 1944.

Dr. Truett was offered the presidency of Baylor University, and in later years he was offered many of the great pastorates of the United States. He had much to do with the starting of Baylor Hospital, the Relief and Annuity Board, and the Southwestern Seminary. Three times he was elected president of the Southern Baptist Convention. He also presided over three sessions of the Baptist World Alliance. His missionary journeys around the world meant much to the cause of Christ. His address at Washington in 1920, before a crowd of twenty thousand, is considered one of the finest statements ever made on the subject for religious liberty. (See pages 110–121.)

6

The Pen in Perspective

Millions of words have been written and thousands of books published by various Baptist authors since the organization of the Triennial Convention in 1814. The process continues and Baptist insights are being shared through the printed word to an ever-widening circle. When one starts reading the contributions of Augustus Strong, William Newton Clarke, Henry Clay Vedder, B. H. Carroll, W. W. Barnes, Kenneth Scott Latourette, W. O. Carver, A. T. Robertson, and countless others who might be named, the reader catches something of the range of materials which are presented. In this chapter we are presenting only selections from Dr. Walter Rauschenbusch and Dr. E. Y. Mullins.

Dr. Rauschenbusch was born on October 4, 1861, in Rochester, New York, where his father was a professor in Rochester Seminary. He attended school in Rochester, in Germany, and for a short time at the Southern Baptist Theological Seminary. He is known chiefly as a writer in the field of sociology; but he was a warmhearted preacher, and much of his concern for social action grew out of his experiences as pastor of the Second German Baptist Church in New York City, in the "Hell's Kitchen" area. For sixteen years he taught church history at Rochester Theological Seminary.

A brief sketch on E. Y. Mullins is presented in the chapter on Baptist pastors. The material presented is from his address at the opening session of the Baptist World Alliance in 1905,

and gives much of his philosophy which was later expanded in
his books.

WALTER RAUSCHENBUSCH

Authoritative Creeds

We have no authoritative creeds to which we pledge the
teachers of our churches. We have never put the future under
bond to the past. In taking the Bible only as our standard, we
have taken as a standard the record of very manifold and
often divergent experiences of God's grace and truth, the
record of a continuous and progressive unfolding of the truth;
thus the very nature of our acknowledged standard pledges us
to a large tolerance and to the maintenance of the spirit of
enquiry. To demand that our ablest and most trusted teachers
shall not go beyond the results of the past, is to darken the
windows through which God may be preparing to shed the
richer light of the coming days. To limit the intellectual field of
our leaders to what is already approved by the mass of men, is
to condemn our denomination to stagnation.

Whether we accept or reject particular results of critical investigation, we assert the right of competent men to investigate
and communicate their results, provided they do both in the
spirit of reverence and of submission to the spirit of truth. We
recognize that there are dangers connected with this right, but
these dangers are inseparable from any stage of transition for
the individual or the church, and Baptists, in parting company
with the traditionalism of the Roman church and the
Jesuit principles in education, have forever avowed that they
prefer the dangers of liberty with the living God to guide them,
to the dangers of intellectual suppression and servility to the
past.

Even if some of us do not belong to it ourselves, we assert
the right of a liberal wing of the Baptist denomination to exist

and to contribute its share to our development. We assert that
the critical investigation of the Bible is the proper function
for a theological professor, if exercised with wisdom and
spiritual insight, and without such wisdom and insight, the
most conservative attitude may be just as deleterious as the
most radical.

Without anger toward anyone we submit these reflections to
all who share in the responsibility of guiding the life of our
denomination. We should feel that our entire denomination
would be involved in guilt if this action were suffered to pass
without protest. The new currents of thought pervading the
life of our times make it probable that similar collisions will
occur elsewhere. To all who endorse this protest we beg that
they will make it as effective as possible by circulating it. To
all who differ from us we give notice that we also are Baptists
and that while we freely yield to the most conservative of our
brethren their abundant opportunities for the assertion of their
views, we shall strenuously vindicate an equal right to ourselves.[1]

Race Relations

We, of the North, have come to realize that the problem of
the black man was solved fifty years ago in anger and bitterness and, therefore, solved very poorly. We realize that we
cannot solve it for the South. But no solution by southern men
can be permanent which does not satisfy the Christian consciousness of the whole nation. And no solution will satisfy the
Christian spirit of our united nation which does not provide for
the progressive awakening of hope and self-respect in the
individual Negro and the awakening of race pride and race
ambition in all Negro communities. We are hearing voices
from the South that practically condemn the black race
permanently to the position of a servile caste, and some that
even deny that the Negro shares the same common human

blood with us. We know well that these views represent only one drift in southern thought, perhaps only a small minority.

But we have before this seen a small oligarchy with determined convictions, and backed by inherited social prejudices and concrete economic interests, swinging great sections of the nation with them and imperiling the moral progress of our people. We owe it to our brethren in the South, who are our beloved kinsmen and one with us, to say that the solution of the problem does not lie that way and never will. Every master class has resented the dawn of independence in a subject class, but the spirit of Pharaoh never works the will of God. However great the practical difficulties may be, the Christian way out is to take our belated black brother by the hand and urge him along the road of steady and intelligent labor, of property rights, of family fidelity, of hope and self-confidence, and of pride and joy in his race achievements, and this work can best be done when North and South join hands in doing it, not ostracizing, but aiding and honoring every one who puts his life alongside of that of the Negro in the spirit of him who never broke the bruised reed or quenched the feeble light of hope, but brought the evangel of freedom and human worth to the poor and backward, and worked miracles through them.[2]

Industrial Relations

We deem it the duty of all Christian people to concern themselves directly with certain practical industrial problems. To us it seems that the churches must stand—

For equal rights and complete justice for all men in all stations of life.

For the right of all men to the opportunity for self-maintenance, a right to be wisely and strongly safe-guarded against encroachments of every kind.

For the right of workers to some protection against the

hardships often resulting from the swift crises of industrial change.

For the principle of conciliation and arbitration in industrial dissensions.

For the protection of the worker from dangerous machinery, occupational disease, injuries, and mortality.

For the abolition of child labor.

For such regulations of the conditions of toil for women as shall safeguard the physical and moral health of the community.

For the suppression of the "sweating system."

For the gradual and reasonable reduction of the hours of labor to the lowest practicable point, and for that degree of leisure for all which is a condition of the highest human life.

For a release from employment one day in seven.

For a living wage as a minimum in every industry, and for the highest wage that each industry can afford.

For the most equitable division of the products of industry that can ultimately be devised.

For suitable provision for the old age of the workers and for those incapacitated by injury.

For the abatement of poverty.

To the toilers of America and to those who by organized effort are seeking to lift the crushing burdens of the poor, and to reduce the hardships and uphold the dignity of labor, this Council sends greetings of human brotherhood and the pledge of sympathy and of help in a cause which belongs to all who follow Christ.[3]

Personal Religion

You ask me to say a word from my heart about personal religion. Perhaps I can state my conviction most effectively by a testimony of my personal experience.

I learned to pray as a little boy at my mother's knee. When

I was leaving boyhood behind me, and the seriousness of life
began to come over me, I felt the call of God, and after a long
struggle extending through several years, I submitted my will
to his law. Henceforth, God was consciously present in my
life, and this gave it a sense of solemnity and worth. This gave
a decisive reinforcement to my will, and turned my life in the
direction of service, and when necessary, self-sacrifice; so
salvation came to me.

But this was only the beginning of my personal religion. It
had to connect with all the chief tasks of my life. When I came
to intellectual maturity I had a second great struggle for
salvation, perhaps of equal spiritual importance. During my
theological education I was confronted with the choice between the imposing authority of human traditions and the self-
evidencing power of God's living word. The former offered
a restful dependence on outward authority; the latter brought
a never ending quest for a holy light that always moved forward. This was the personal religious problem of faith applied
to intellectual duty. I now had to lean back on the living
spirit of God for support in my intellectual work, and felt his
co-operation. This extended the area of personal religion in my
life. I am inexpressibly grateful that I made the choice aright.

In my effort to secure more freedom and justice for men I
acted under religious impulses. I realize that God hates in-
justice and that I would be quenching the life of God within
me if I kept silent with all this social iniquity of the world
around me.

My life has been physically very lonely and often beset by
the consciousness of conservative antagonism. I have been up-
held by the comforts of God. Jesus has been to me the inex-
haustible source of fresh impulses, life and courage.

My life would seem an empty shell if my personal religion
were left out of it. It has been my deepest satisfaction to get
evidence now and then that I have been able to help men to a

new spiritual birth. I have always regarded my public work as
a form of evangelism, which called for a deeper repentance
and a new experience of God's salvation.[4]

E. Y. MULLINS

The Theological Trend

If we consider the Christian centuries as a whole, we may
distinguish the great leading types of theology into four and
four only. The first of these is the Latin or Augustinian type,
which construes all theological truth around the idea of God
as Sovereign. It received its earliest commanding statement at
the hands of the great bishop of Hippo. This theology, revived
and made current by John Calvin, has beyond all others ruled
in the theological realm since the Reformation. The second is
the Greek type of theology, which sought in particular to
reconcile Christianity and culture. Its structural principle was
the human consciousness, man's sense of freedom and original
likeness to God. Under the vitalising hand of Clement of
Alexandria, Origen and others, in the early centuries, revived
and made current again by Schleiermacher in modern times,
this type of theology has gained a currency in our day beyond
that of any period in the past. A third type of theology is the
sacramental, which economises all doctrine around the conception of the sacraments. In the Roman Church through many
centuries, and in the Oxford movement in more recent times,
it has asserted its power in the Christian World. The fourth
type may be designated the theology of the inner life, which
has received its chief development in the writings of the
Christian mystics at intervals throughout the Christian ages. Its
starting point is Christian experience, or the soul in direct
relations with God through Christ and the Spirit.

All these types of theology are important factors in the thinking of men today. All of them claim the support of the Scrip-

tures, in greater or less degree. They are not, of course, always sharply defined and mutually exclusive. But as conflicting principles, or as presenting materials for fresh combination and larger synthesis, they include within themselves all the essential interests which may be described as strictly and essentially theological.

[The major part of this address dealt with the four "imperious necessities" which were then influencing theological thought: the religious, the ethical, the apologetic, and the metaphysical. Dr. Mullins easily demonstrated his grasp of the theological issues of his day and brought his hearers to consider the following ideas that would shape all his later writing and teaching.]

The critical questions which remain in the theology of today are concerned with the following: the basis and nature of religious authority, the deity of Christ and His atoning work, the nature of sin, and the general relations of theology to social questions.

Behind these questions lie the philosophic issues between Christian theism and antitheistic theories, and . . . the question of the reality and nature of knowledge.

I must now forecast briefly the probable course of theological reconstruction in the light of the above considerations. Theology, then, in the future will not adopt rationalism as its constructive principle, because rationalism is not always compatible with the interests of life. Naturalism also, which fails altogether to yield a theology in the proper sense, will be avoided, for the reason that it is incapable of coping with the situation created by sin. Evolution, while containing a relative truth as to physical nature, breaks down in the attempt to explain the phenomena and facts of the personal and social realm. A merely deistic conception of God is, of course, to be

discarded as inadequate. The doctrine of the Divine imma-
nence alone cannot serve as a sufficient principle of theological
reconstruction, because it inevitably merges God in nature and
in man, and tends to pull the entire structure down to the level
of naturalism.

Positively stated, the best theology of the future will continue to accept the authority of the Scriptures, but it will take
as its starting-point, for the interpretation and illumination of
Scripture, the facts of Christian experience, not in a single
aspect, but in their totality. First, because Christian experience,
thus employed, conforms to the scientific ideal which above all
things seeks to know the facts of nature, life and religion, and
resents theoretical constructions apart from experience in the
realm of facts. It conforms, second, to the true philosophical
ideal, which also demands a fact basis for all the speculative
attempts of the intellect. Thirdly, experience will also restore
with greatly increased power the older arguments from the
cosmos for the existence of God, transferred in part, however,
from the cosmos of nature to the cosmos of the inner life.
Fourthly, experience will sustain the cause of the supernatural
in its collision with naturalism, because it brings contact with
the supernatural in consciousness the most indubitable of all
the spheres of reality. In the fifth place, experience will in increasing measure establish the validity of the vicarious atone-
ment of Christ, and its corresponding doctrines of sin and of
Christ's deity and present action upon men. Thus it will indirectly add an important contribution to the doctrine of the
Trinity. It will also affirm, and at the same time limit and define, the reality of knowledge of transcendental objects in the
religious sphere, and indirectly rejuvenate the weakened convictions of an agnostic science in the realm of material research. Sixth, theological dogma will increasingly become the
dogma of conviction, as opposed to the dogma of mere
authority.

Thus, the confusions and contradictions in recent writers on authority, as of Sabatier, for example, will be dispelled. The externalists and internalists on authority will discover a larger truth than either theory. Christ's authority will be seen to be real, but incapable of adequate statement save as a paradox. Christ is man's final authority in religion, because He imparts spiritual autonomy to man. Man, who is made in God's image, finds in the truth of Christ the ideal of his own higher moral self. Man realises in and through Christ his own ideal independence. He is thus eternally a subject and eternally free. Authority in religion will remain external so long as there is a reserve of life and truth in Christ, but that authority is forever in process of becoming internal, as men appropriate Christ. Experience will vindicate the authority of the Scriptures, for the experience of God through Christ and the Spirit is seen to be the real inner bond of unity in all the course of revelation. Scripture as a record of original experience cannot be transcended, nor can it lose its authority; for the sufficient reason that to discard Scripture is to discard the only means of understanding the historic Christ who emancipates man and imparts to him spiritual autonomy. Faith expires in a vacuum without contact with the historic Christ of Scripture as well as the risen and ascended and living Christ.

Again, experience will guide in the final construction of the doctrine of God for the reason that experience reaches its conception of God, not through nature, but through man, nature's crown; and not merely through the natural man, but through the supernatural and Divine Man, Jesus Christ. It will also appear, as experience grows, that in its Christian form it gathers together as in a focus all that is valid and universal in man's quest for God. It will at once thus discredit and fulfil the ethnic types of experience, by showing their inadequacy to man's needs on the one hand, and on the other that it is the answer of God in Christ to man's age-long endeavour to find

God. Christian experience, then, will appear as the universal religious and moral ultimate for man, short of which it is impossible for religious experience to halt, and beyond which it is impossible to proceed.

Now, the relation of Baptists to this great theological movement has not been adequately recognised and needs defining afresh. Behind our contentions as to baptism and communion and related topics lie a group of great and elemental principles. These principles are religious ultimates, nay, they are axioms, which the instructed religious consciousness of man cannot repudiate. I sum them up and submit them as a statement of the basis at once for a new Baptist apologetic and a platform for universal adoption.

1. The theological axiom: *The holy and loving God has a right to be Sovereign.* Time forbids that I elaborate this statement in its implications as to the incarnation, and as to Christianity as the religion of the Divine initiative.

2. The religious axiom: *All men have an equal right to direct access to God.* This principle is fatal to the practice of infant baptism and to the idea of a human priesthood.

3. The ecclesiastical axiom: *All believers have equal privileges in the Church.* Hierarchies and centralised authorities disappear under the operation of this principle.

4. The moral axiom: *To be responsible man must be free.* This is an elemental truth which cannot receive thoroughgoing application save where ecclesiastical bonds of mere authority are absent.

5. The social axiom: *Love your neighbour as yourself.* This makes the Kingdom of God the goal of the social movement.

6. The religio-civic axiom: *A free Church in a free State.* For this principle Baptists have ever stood. Without it the future of theology and of the Church is fraught with extreme peril.

These axioms are the predestined goal of man's religious

thinking. They spring out of Scripture teaching, they meet a deep response in Christian experience. When understood they commend themselves as the universal and necessary and self-evident forms of man's religious life. They are deep like the ocean, elastic and free as the life-giving atmosphere which enswathes the earth, and expansive and comprehensive as the overarching sky. For them the Baptists stand. Planting ourselves upon them our position cannot be successfully assailed. By means of them Baptists will make fruitful the course of theological development in the ages to come.

---

[1] Letter. Quoted by D. R. Sharpe, *Walter Rauschenbusch* (New York: The Macmillan Co., 1942), pp. 106–7.

[2] Walter Rauschenbusch, *The Belated Race and the Social Problem.* American Missionary Association.

[3] Quoted by D. R. Sharpe, *op. cit.,* from "The Social Creed of the Churches," edited by Harry F. Ward.

[4] Letter to L. C. Barnes. Quoted by Sharpe, *ibid.,* pp. 434–5.

7

For Liberty and Light

Both church and state are ordained of God and are answerable to him. Each is distinct; each has a divine purpose; neither is to encroach upon the rights of the other. They are to remain separate, but they are to stand in proper relationship with each other under God. The state is ordained of God for the exercise of civil authority, the maintenance of order, and the promotion of public welfare.

The church is a voluntary fellowship of Christians, joined together under the lordship of Christ for worship and service in his name. The state is not to ignore God's sovereignty or reject his laws as the basis for moral order and social justice. Christians are to accept their responsibilities for the support of the state and for loyal obedience to civil authorities in all things not contrary to the clear will of God.

The state owes the church protection and full freedom in the pursuit of its spiritual ends. The church owes the state moral and spiritual reinforcement for law and order and the clear proclamation of those truths which undergird justice and peace. The church is responsible both to pray for the state and to declare the judgments of God as they relate to government, responsible citizenship, and the rights of all persons. The church must take seriously and practice consistently the principles which it declares should govern the relation of church and state.

This statement from *Baptist Ideals* was prepared by a committee of Southern Baptist leaders and scholars and deals with one of the characteristic contributions of Baptists in the life of our nation.

Many sermons have been preached on the relationship of

the church and the state, but two of the best known are the sermons preached by Dr. George Dana Boardman on Thanksgiving Day in the First Baptist Church in Philadelphia, 1881, and by Dr. George W. Truett on the steps of the capitol during the session of the Southern Baptist Convention held in Washington in 1920.

George Dana Boardman was born in Burma in 1828 and became the stepson of Adoniram Judson. After studies at Brown he felt he wanted to study law but then answered the call to the ministry and graduated from Newton Theological Institution in 1855. He became pastor of the First Baptist Church of Philadelphia where he remained until his death. He was considered one of the outstanding ministers among American Baptists.

A sketch on Dr. Truett's life is presented in Chapter 5.

These sermons are reproduced here in part and with incidental changes in form. The Truett sermon was distributed in tract form for many years by the Sunday School Board.

THE TWO ANOINTED ONES:
or
CHURCH AND STATE

George Dana Boardman

[Dr. Boardman used Zechariah 4:11–14 as his text and began the sermon with a review of setting of the prophet's vision. He argued that the two olive trees were symbolic of the two orders: church and state. Then he turned to Matthew 22:15–22 to consider Jesus' reply to the tribute question.]

I. *Render to Caesar Caesar's Things*

And, first: "Render unto Caesar the things which are Caesar's." Then, according to Jesus Christ, Caesar does have his things. And having them, they must be rendered unto him. The origin of Civil Government is a problem which has baffled the ingenuity of subtile intellects in every age. The principal theories in this matter may be reduced to two. The first theory—recognizing Civil Government as an external fact, existing independent of men's wills—traces its origin back to the Paternal or Patriarchal system of rule. This was the view maintained by the Tories and the great body of Churchmen under the English Stuarts, and on which they founded their famous doctrines of the divine right of Kings, and of passive obedience, or absolute nonresistance. The second theory regarding Civil Government as a creature of men's wills—represents it as a Social Contract. Just as two or more men unite together for certain purposes of business, and pledge themselves to obey certain rules mutually agreed upon, which rules are binding so long as the contract stands, so Civil Government is conceived of as a compact between each and every citizen.

This is the common theory. Thus the Parliament which deposed James II declared by solemn vote that James had "broken the original contract between King and People." Thus also we read in the Constitution of Massachusetts: "The body politic is formed by a voluntary association of individuals: it is a social compact by which the whole people covenants with each citizen, and each citizen with the whole people, that all shall be governed by certain laws for the common good." Now, this theory, as you perceive at once, does not explain at all the origin of Civil Government. Besides, it would be a difficult matter for even the astutest lawyer to ascertain the day on which you and I, as citizens of the United States, entered into any such contract, or to state the terms of the contract we agreed upon; to say nothing of the fact that Government has rights which no contract among the subjects can confer. The theory is, as the old schoolmen would have said, a simple *ens rationis,* or creature of reason. Yet, like some other figments of law, as, for instance, "The State is a person," "The King never dies," this theory, that Civil Government is a social compact, has certain advantages; it is a convenient form for expressing political and legal principles.

Now, Holy Scripture cuts short all these speculations by positively asserting that Civil Government is of Divine origin, and consequently of Divine authority, and this it asserts in the broadest term; for, while it explicitly defines the duty of the subject, it does not define the nature or structure of the particular government to which that duty is owing.

[Dr. Boardman then quoted Romans 13:1–7 and recalled Acts 16:19–39 and 22:24–25 to show that early Christian leaders insisted that believers should be obedient to the government even in days of persecution.]

First.—Civil Government is a Divine institution: "Let everyone submit himself to the higher powers: for there is no power but of God; and the powers that be are ordained of God." That is to say: We are to accept Government as a divine fact, which exists as soon as, and wherever, men exist. There never has been a nation so degraded that it had no government. There has never been a nation so advanced that it intentionally based its government on the idea of a social compact, except as a figment of law. Men never have lived, and men never will live, and this simply because men never can live, without government. Government is a divine fact; just as light, or gravitation, or man himself is a divine fact. God created light; God established the principle of gravitation; God brings man into being; God makes government. We shall never be able to trace the origin or basis of Civil Government farther back than was done more than two thousand years ago, by the great philosopher of Stagira: "It is manifest," says Aristotle, "that the State is one of the things which exist by nature, and that man in virtue of his very being, is a political animal." And a greater than Aristotle has declared, as in our passage: "The authorities which exist have been ordained by God." That is to say: the fact of Civil Government is not a creature of human will; it is a divine institution, existing wherever men exist. Accordingly the question is not one *de jure;* the question is one *de facto*.

These who are in authority are to be obeyed within their sphere, no matter how or by whom appointed; and this because Civil Government is a divine ordinance. The powers that be are ordained of God; not because they chance to have been justly installed; not because they chance at present to be justly administered: but because they are the Government; and Government is a divine institution. Or, to recur to Zechariah's vision, Civic Authority is one of the two olive trees or anointed ones that stand before the Lord of the whole earth. For, according to the divinely ordained custom for Israel, kings, not less than priests, on their inauguration, received the sacred unction, or anointing, from the Lord. In this very passage of Paul to the Romans he three times speaks of magistrates as being God's "ministers."

Again: Resistance to Government is resistance to God; "Whosoever, therefore, resisteth the authority, resisteth what God has ordained."

And now you burst upon me with a question: "If the powers that be are ordained of God, and if whoever resists the powers resists the ordinance of God, how then can revolutions ever be justified? What redress have we when tyranny becomes absolutely intolerable? Will you carry your doctrine of loyalty to the extreme of pronouncing, for instance, our own American Revolution an act of treason rather than of patriotism?"

[Dr. Boardman attempted to give a serious answer to these questions, arguing that revolutions are exceptional cases and are never justified until every "means of constitutional redress has been exhausted." With two illustrations—killing in self-defense and whether a child is ever right in disobeying his parents—he showed that "the line which separates the patriot from the traitor is sometimes very narrow and delicate."]

Again: Since Civil Government is of divine origin and authority, we, as Christians, should cheerfully sustain it with our pecuniary and moral support: "For this cause, pay tribute also; for they are ministers of God's service, attending continually upon this very business: render to all their dues; tribute to whom tribute is due; custom, to whom custom; fear, to whom fear; honor, to whom honor." In other words participation in civic affairs or politics is a religious duty, and this because Civil Government is a divine institution. And if this was true under the despotism of the Caesars, how much truer under a democracy! Of the American State it may be more truly said than of any other nation: "We are members one of another." The sphere for the perfection of national character is not the monastery, but the polling-place. See to it, then, my countrymen, what kind of men those are who are nominated for public office. The disgrace and crime of our American politics is this: our rulers, practically speaking, are elected, not by the citizens, but by venal tricksters in the primaries and jobbing nominees at the polls. Thank God, a brighter day seems to be dawning. Not that I would court cheap applause by joining in every hue and cry for "Reform," even pirates may sometimes flaunt an honest flag. But signs are not wanting that the American people are waking to the fact that there is something nobler than to be a party man: it is to be a free man. Nominate, then, for office, I implore you, our best men, whether Republicans or Democrats, incumbents or reformers. Elect none but men of unquestioned personal probity; men who scorn bribery in whatever direction it approaches, or however innocent the guise it assumes; men who have the courage of personal convictions; men whose instincts, as well as professions, are on the side of honesty, and equity, and temperance, and purity, and brotherhood, and reverence; men who, like the statesman Daniel in Babylon, dare to be seen kneeling with their faces toward Jerusalem. This is the great demand of our times. We want to see in this last quarter of the nineteenth century of our Lord, and of the independence of the United States the one hundred and fifth year, Christian statesmen, who, like our lamented Garfield, dare bring the principles of the gospel of Jesus Christ into the arena of politics. We want to see legislation conceived and executed in the spirit of the Lord of Souls. We want to see in our executive chairs, national, and State, and municipal; in our cabinets; in our congresses, and legislatures, and city councils; on our seats of tribunal, men who fear God, and keep His commandments; men who dare to make the Star-Spangled Banner not merely the symbol of unstained honor and commercial integrity and universal liberty and generous education and national glory; but also the symbol of Christian civilization, and a beacon to the cross of the Galilean. Then shall the voice of the people be indeed the voice of God.

II. Render to God God's Things

And so we are prepared for our second lesson: "Render unto God the things that are God's." Then God, not less than Caesar, does have also His things. And having them, they must be rendered unto Him. While Caesar, or Civil Government, is a divine ordinance, being a minister of God's service, so also is His Church, in virtue of her being the representative of His Son Jesus Christ. The Church of the living God is the other of the two olive trees, or anointed ones, that stand before the Lord of the whole earth. But it is not needful that I argue this point, as I did the other; for it is the warm confession and meek boast of all Christians that the Church of Immanuel is in an eminent sense a divine institution.

Nevertheless, I would loiter for a moment to press this duty of rendering unto God the things that are God's, not less than

unto Caesar the things that are Caesar's. My countrymen, I fear
that we are better patriots than Christians. You denounced the
late rebellion, and put forth your sublime might to crush it,
and, I thank God, you succeeded. You demanded that Caesar
should have his things, and Caesar, by the might of your prow-
ess, did receive them, but how about your rendering unto God
the things that are God's? For He is the King of kings, the Lord
of lords. Will you be loyal to Caesar and disloyal to Caesar's
Caesar? "But wherein have we been disloyal to God?" you ask
me. Let me answer in the words of an ancient prophet: "Will a
man rob God? Yet ye rob Me, saith the Lord of hosts. And ye
say: 'Wherein do we rob Thee?' In the tithes and the offerings;
ye rob Me, even this whole nation" (Mal. 3:8–9). Do you feel
this to be an unjust charge? Ponder then this one fact out of
many similar ones: Although we profess to be a Christian nation, devoting our all to Jesus Christ, yet, for every one dollar
we put into His treasury, we put a million into our own. For,
friend, who lent you that property? who bestowed on you that
capacity? who blesses you with health? who spares you from
moment to moment? . . .

But let me resume my argument. Although the Church, as
being God's representative in the world, is like the State, a
divine institution, yet the two institutions are, or at least were
divinely meant to be entirely distinct.

III. Separation of Church and State

And so we pass to our third lesson: The separation of
Church and State. Recall the prophet's vision of the golden
candlestick: while there was but one chandelier, there were
two olive trees; while each emptied the oil out of itself, through
its own golden pipe, into the common reservoir, on the top of
the lamp-stand, the two trees stood apart, the one on the right
of the candelabrum, the other on the left.

It is a great lesson for all those devout spirits who, in their

longing for the speedy triumph of Christianity, would crave
the alliance of the State. That the Church should be enthroned
as the confessed mistress of the world; that she should visibly
wield its civic powers, dictating its rulers, and legislations, and
policies; that the mitre and the crown should encircle the same
brow, and that brow her own, so that where the crozier had
failed the scimitar should not; that emperors should be her
chosen patrons and defenders, and her throne be borne in
resplendent state on the shoulders of princes: this has always
been a favorite dream of many of God's chosen ones. The
dream of such a City of God especially beguiled the flaming
heart of the great Augustine.

But such a dream has ever led into peril. Would God that
the Church had always profited by the story of Satan's temptation of Jesus on the mountain. (Matt. iv, 7–10.) In the secu-
larizing of Christianity by the allying of Church and State; in
the smothering the spirituality of Christ's kingdom by the
patronage and championship of political sovereignties; in the
soiling her purity and the fettering her energies by the selfish
and slippery policies of state-craft; in the invoking the arm of
the civil power to maintain and propagate her faith; in the
decreeing that non-conformity to her ritual shall be heresy, and
liberty of conscience shall be treason; in the opening of Parliament chambers to her mitred dignitaries; in the filling earth's
cabinets with her cardinals and legates and nuncios; in the en-
riching her coffers with the levies of her fiefs, and the tolls of
her imperial lieges; in her cross and keys emblazoned on
senate-house and post-office; in the cannonading of her St.
Angelo on Easter morning; in the insisting that the word "God"
or "Christ" shall be inserted in the National Constitution; in
brief, in the demanding legislation in behalf of the Church:
in all this we see the devil's victory over the Church at pre-
cisely the point where the devil was vanquished by the
Church's Master.

And as the devil promised to Jesus that he would give Him all the kingdoms of the world, and the glory of them if He would but make His own kingdom a worldly one, so he has often fulfilled that promise in the case of those who have yielded to his temptation. But his gifts have proved to be satanic gifts indeed. As long as the Church insisted on the spirituality of Christ's kingdom, while as yet her ministers went forth without purse or sword, preaching that kingdom which is not food and drink, but righteousness, and peace, and joy in the Holy (Rom. xiv, 17.) Ghost; so long was the Church comparatively pure in doctrine and in practice. But when her success began to arrest the attention of the rulers of this world, and they saw that her influence was to be courted, and when she yielded to their seductive proffers of aid; then a tide of impurity began to set in which ere long submerged her in all manner of filth and abomination. The most ominous day the Church ever saw was the day when Constantine the Great, having renounced heathenism, proclaimed himself the imperial patron of Christianity and defender of the Faith. That alliance of Church and State set back the Church for centuries, and to this day she is reeling beneath the satanic stab she then received. Ay, it was Church and State, Caiaphas and Pilate, that crucified the Lord of Glory. . . .

IV. Reticulation of Church and State

Nevertheless, we are to learn in this connection a fourth important lesson: It is the interrelation of Church and State. Although there were two olive trees, the one standing on the right of the golden candelabrum, and the other on the left, yet they both had golden ducts through which they emptied the oil out of themselves into the common reservoir surmounting the golden chandelier. Church and State are separate, yet they have a common mission, and a common focus: supply of oil for the one candlestick of Christ's kingdom. The relation of

Church and State is not the chemical union of hydrogen and oxygen in a molecule of water; it is the local mixture of nitrogen and oxygen in a molecule of air. Or, to take a better illustration from organic life, the relation of Church and State is not the vital union of spirit and body, but the corporate relation of the two arms in the one body; the Church serving as God's right hand, and the State as God's left. Church and State, in their ideal workings, are absolutely distinct, yet mutually reticulate, forming one warp and woof in God's scheme for human redemption. The high-priest Aaron and the legislator Moses, the prophet Ezekiel and the statesman Daniel, the pontiff Joshua and the governor Zerubbabel—these are the two anointed one, who stand before the Lord of the whole earth.

Brethren, it is cause for justest felicitation that, among the many noble champions of a Christianity unentangled by State alliances, the foremost and bravest have been those who were identified with our own faith and order. At the very time that Puritan John Knox was proclaiming the right of the civil magistrate to prosecute those whom he called heretics because they were not Presbyterians, Baptist Churches in Great Britain, Germany, and Holland were protesting against all prosecutions whatever, grounded on conscientious divergence. At the very time Puritan John Robinson was maintaining the power of the civil magistrate to compel every member of the community to join himself to a Christian church, Baptist John Smyth opposed him, declaring that the magistrate had no right to "meddle with matters of conscience, or compel men to this or that form of religion, because Christ is the king and lawgiver of the church and conscience." At the very time that the Puritan fathers were banishing from Massachusetts Bay all who would not subscribe to their articles of faith, Baptist Roger Williams, himself one of the banished ones, was heroically proclaiming his doctrine of soul-liberty, and founding a political commonwealth, which, for the first time in the history of the American Church, incorporated among its fundamental principles absolute freedom of conscience, and total separation of Church and State. In 1815 the Philadelphia Association met with our own First Baptist Church. Dr. William Staughton was moderator, and Dr. H. G. Jones, clerk. Among those present were two of my illustrious predecessors in the pastoral office, Dr. William Rogers and Dr. Henry Holcombe. In the course of the sessions, Rev. James Patterson, a member of the Sansom Street Church, presented "a communication from their Presbyterian brethren, respecting the profanation of the Lord's Day, and requesting the co-operation of their Society to procure, by legislative interference, a more strict observance of the same." The Association thereupon

Resolved, That this Association, acting upon principles which have guided them, and which they hope ever to hold sacred—principles which lead them to regard every exercise of civil power to enforce the institutions of religions, as the assumption of an illegitimate prerogative, cannot as a religious body make any application to the legislature upon that subject; but being with their brethern deeply sensible of the disgrace brought upon the community, by the practice of which they complain, as an outrage against divine authority, and confirmed by experience in the opinion, that such conduct is detrimental to the best interests of civil society; they recommend as Christians and as patriots to every member of the churches in connection with them, that they seek the redress of this grievance by every means arising to them from the social compact which may not infringe upon religious liberty; and labor all to illustrate and enforce by their conduct as citizens of this commonwealth and citizens of Zion, the propriety and the beauty, the social good and the blessedness which must result from the due observance of a day ordained by the wisest and the best of Legislators.

All this I say, brethren, not in any spirit of sectarian boasting, but in fidelity to the facts of history.

Let us then, as American Christians, thank God for the

Church; for the State; for the separation of Church and State;
for the co-operation of Church and State as ministers of God's
service. . . .

BAPTISTS AND RELIGIOUS LIBERTY

George W. Truett

[After a brief introduction Dr. Truett launched into a discussion of his central thesis.]

We shall do well, both as citizens and as Christians, if we
hark back to the chief actors and lessons in the early and
epoch-making struggles of this great Western democracy, for
the full establishment of civil and religious liberty—back to the
days of Washington and Jefferson and Madison, and back to
the days of our Baptist fathers, who paid such a great price
through the long generations, that liberty, both religious and
civil, might have free course and be glorified everywhere.

Years ago, at a notable dinner in London, that world-famed
statesman, John Bright, asked an American statesman, himself
a Baptist, the noble Dr. J. L. M. Curry, "What distinct contribution has your America made to the science of government?" To that question Dr. Curry replied: "The doctrine of
religious liberty." After a moment's reflection, Mr. Bright made
the worthy reply: "It was a tremendous contribution."

Indeed, the supreme contribution of the new world to the
old is the contribution of religious liberty. This is the chiefest
contribution that America has thus far made to civilization.
And historic justice compels us to say that it was pre-eminently
a Baptist contribution. The impartial historian, whether in the
past, present or future, will ever agree with our American
historian, Mr. Bancroft, when he says: "Freedom of conscience,

unlimited freedom of mind, was from the first the trophy of the Baptists." And such historian will concur with the noble John Locke who said: "The Baptists were the first propounders of absolute liberty, just and true liberty, equal and impartial liberty." Ringing testimonies like these might be multiplied indefinitely.

Not Toleration, but Right

Baptists have one consistent record concerning liberty throughout all their long and eventful history. They have never been party to oppression of conscience. They have ever been the unwavering champions of liberty, both religious and civil. Their contention now is, and has been, and please God, must ever be, that it is the natural and fundamental and indefeasible right of every human being to worship God or not, according to the dictates of his conscience, and as long as he does not infringe upon the rights of others, he is to be held accountable alone to God for all religious beliefs and practices. Our contention is not for mere toleration, but for absolute liberty. There is a wide difference between toleration and liberty. Toleration implies that somebody falsely claims the right to tolerate. Toleration is a concession, while liberty is a right. Toleration is a matter of expediency, while liberty is a matter of principle. Toleration is a gift from man, while liberty is a gift from God. It is the consistent and insistent contention of our Baptist people, always and everywhere, that religion must be forever voluntary and uncoerced, and that it is not the prerogative of any power, whether civil or ecclesiastical, to compel men to conform to any religious creed or form of worship, or to pay taxes for the support of a religious organization to which they do not believe. God wants free worshippers and no other kind.

What is the explanation of this consistent and notably praiseworthy record of our plain Baptist people in the realm of religious liberty? The answer is at hand. It is not because Baptists are inherently better than their neighbours—we would make no such arrogant claim. Happy are our Baptist people to live side by side with their neighbours of other Christian faiths and to have fellowship with such neighbours, and to honor such servants of God for their inspiring lives and their noble deeds. From our deepest hearts we pray: "Grace be with all them that love our Lord Jesus Christ in sincerity." The spiritual union of all true believers in Christ is now and ever will be a blessed reality, and such union is deeper and higher and more enduring than any and all forms and rituals and organizations. Whoever believes in Christ as his personal Saviour is our brother in the common salvation, whether he be a member of one communion or of another, or of no communion at all.

How is it, then, that Baptists, more than any other people in the world, have forever been the protagonists of religious liberty, and its compatriot, civil liberty? They did not stumble upon this principle. Their uniform, unyielding and sacrificial advocacy of such principle was not and is not an accident. It is, in a word, because of our essential and fundamental principles. Ideas rule the world. A denomination is moulded by its ruling principles, just as a nation is thus moulded and just as individual life is thus moulded. Our fundamental essential principles have made our Baptist people, of all ages and countries, to be the unyielding protagonists of religious liberty, not only for themselves, but as well for everybody else.

Such fact at once provokes the inquiry: What are these fundamental Baptist principles which compel Baptists in Europe, in America, in some far-off seagirt island, to be forever contending for unrestricted religious liberty? First of all, and explaining all the rest, is the doctrine of absolute Lordship of Jesus Christ. That doctrine is for Baptists the dominant fact in all their Christian experience, the nerve center of all their Christian life, the bedrock of all their church polity, the sheet anchor of all their hopes, the climax and crown of all their rejoicings. They say with Paul: "For to this end Christ both died and rose again, that he might be Lord both of the dead and the living."

From that germinal conception of the absolute Lordship of Christ, all our Baptist principles emerge. Just as yonder oak came from the acorn, so our many-branched Baptist life came from the cardinal principle of the absolute Lordship of Christ. The Christianity of our Baptist people, from Alpha to Omega, lives and moves and has its whole being in the realm of the doctrine of the Lordship of Christ. "One is your Master, even Christ, and all ye are brethren." Christ is the one head of the church. All authority has been committed unto Him, in heaven and on earth, and he must be given the absolute pre-eminence in all things. One clear note is ever to be sounded concerning Him, even this, "Whatsoever He saith unto you, do it."

The Bible Our Rule of Faith and Practice

How shall we find out Christ's will for us? He has revealed it in His Holy Word. The Bible and the Bible alone is the rule of faith and practice for Baptists. To them the one standard by which all creeds and conduct and character must be tried is the Word of God. They ask only one question concerning all religious faith and practice, and that question is, "What saith the Word of God?" Not traditions, nor customs, nor councils, nor confessions, nor ecclesiastical formularies, however venerable and pretentious, guide Baptists, but simply and solely the will of Christ as they find it revealed in the New Testament. The immortal B. H. Carroll has thus stated it for us: "The New Testament is the law of Christianity. All the New Testament is the law of Christianity. The New Testament is all the law of Christianity. The New Testament will always be all the law of Christianity."

Baptists hold that this law of Christianity, the Word of God, is the unchangeable and only law of Christ's reign, and that whatever is not found in the law cannot be bound on the consciences of men, and that this law is a sacred deposit, an inviolable trust, which Christ's friends are commissioned to guard and perpetuate wherever it may lead and whatever may be the cost of such trusteeship.

. . . .

The Present Call

And now, my fellow Christians, and fellow citizens, what is the present call to us in connection with the priceless principle of religious liberty? That principle, with all the history and heritage accompanying it, imposes upon us obligations to the last degree meaningful and responsible. Let us today and forever be highly resolved that the principle of religious liberty shall, please God, be preserved inviolate through all our days and the days of those who come after us. Liberty has both its perils and its obligations. We are to see to it that our attitude toward liberty, both religious and civil, both as Christians and as citizens, is an attitude consistent and constructive and worthy. We are to "Render unto Caesar the things that are Caesar's, and unto God the things that are God's." We are members of the two realms, the civil and the religious, and we are faithfully to render unto each all that each should receive at our hands; we are to be alertly watchful, day and night, that liberty, both religious and civil, shall be nowhere prostituted and mistreated. Every perversion and misuse of liberty tends by that much to jeopardize both church and state.

There comes now the clarion call to us to be the right kind of citizens. Happily, the record of our Baptist people toward civil government has been a record of unfading honour. Their love and loyalty to country have not been put to shame in any land. In the long list of published Tories in connection with the Revolutionary War there was not one Baptist name.

It behooves us now and ever to see to it that liberty is not abused. Well may we listen to the call of Paul, that mightiest Christian of the long centuries, as he said: "Brethren, ye have been called unto liberty; only use not liberty for an occasion to the flesh, but by love serve one another." This ringing declaration should be heard and heeded by every class and condition of people throughout all our wide-stretching nation.

It is the word to be heeded by religious teachers, by editors, and by legislators, and by everybody else. Nowhere is liberty to be used "for an occasion to the flesh." We will take free speech and a free press, with all their excrescences and perils, because of the high meaning of freedom, but we are to set ourselves with all diligence not to use these great privileges in the shaming of liberty. A free press—how often does it pervert its high privilege! Again and again, it may be seen dragging itself through all the sewers of the social order, bringing to light the moral cancers and leprosies of our poor world and glaringly exhibiting them to the gaze even of responsive youth and childhood. The editor's task, whether in the realm of church or state, is an immeasurably responsible one. These editors, side by side with the moral and religious teachers of the country are so to magnify the ballot box, a free press, free schools, the courts, the majesty of law and reverence for all properly accredited authority that our civilization may not be built on the shifting sands, but on the secure and enduring foundations of righteousness.

Let us remember that lawlessness, wherever found and whatever its form, is as the pestilence that walketh in darkness and the destruction that wasteth at noonday. Let us remember that he who is willing for law to be violated is an offender against the majesty of law as really as he who actually violates law. The spirit of law is the spirit of civilization. Liberty without law is anarchy. Liberty against law is rebellion. Liberty limited by law is the formula of civilization.

Challenging to the highest degree is the call that comes to legislators. They are to see to it continually, in all their legislative efforts, that their supreme concern is for the highest welfare of the people. Laws humane and righteous are to be fashioned and then to be faithfully enforced. Men are playing with fire if they lightly fashion their country's laws and then trifle in their obedience to such laws. Indeed, all citizens, the humblest and the most prominent alike, are called to give their best thought to the maintenance of righteousness everywhere. Much truth is there in the widely quoted saying: "Our country is afflicted with the bad citizenship of good men." The saying points its own clear lesson. "When the righteous are in authority, the people rejoice, but when the wicked bear rule, the people mourn." The people, all the people, are inexorably responsible for the laws, the ideals, and the spirit that are necessary for the making of a great and enduring civilization. Every man of us is to remember that it is righteousness that exalteth a nation, and that it is sin that reproaches and destroys a nation.

God does not raise up a nation to go selfishly strutting and forgetful of the high interests of humanity. National selfishness leads to destruction as truly as does individual selfishness. Nations can no more live to themselves than can individuals. Humanity is bound up together in the big bundle of life. The world is now one big neighbourhood. There are no longer any hermit nations. National isolation is no longer possible in the earth. The markets of the world instantly register every commercial change. An earthquake in Asia is at once registered in Washington City. The people on one side of the world may not dare to be indifferent to the people on the other side. Every man of us is called to be a world citizen and to think and act in world terms. The nation that insists upon asking that old murderous question of Cain, "Am I my brother's keeper?," the question of the profiteer and the question of the slacker, is a nation marked for decay and doom and death. The parable of the good Samaritan is heaven's law for nations as well as for individuals. Some things are worth dying for, and if they are worth dying for they are worth living for. . . .

Things Worth Dying For

When this nation went into the world war a little while ago, after her long and patient and fruitless effort to find another way of conserving righteousness, the note was sounded in every nook and corner of our country that some things in this world are worth dying for, and if they are worth dying for they are worth living for. What are some of the things worth dying for? The sanctity of womanhood is worth dying for. The safety of childhood is worth dying for, and when Germany put to death that first helpless Belgian child she was marked for defeat and doom. The integrity of one's country is worth dying for. And, please God, the freedom and honour of the United States of America are worth dying for. If the great things of life are worth dying for, they are surely worth living for. Our great country may not dare to isolate herself from the rest of the world, and selfishly say: "We propose to live and to die to ourselves, leaving all the other nations with their weaknesses and burdens and sufferings to go their ways without our help." This nation cannot pursue any such policy and expect the favour of God. Myriads of voices, both from the living and the dead, summon us to a higher and better way. Happy am I to believe that God has his prophets not only in the pulpits of the churches but also in the school room, in the editor's chair, in the halls of legislation, in marts of commerce, in the realms of literature. . . .

Tennyson believed in a league of nations, and well might he so believe, because God is on his righteous throne, and inflexible are his purposes touching righteousness and peace for a weary, sinning, suffering, dying world. Standing here today on the steps of our Nation's capitol, hard by the chamber of the

Senate of the United States, I dare to say as a citizen and as a Christian teacher, that the moral forces of the United States of America, without regard to political parties, will never rest until there is a worthy League of Nations. I dare to express also the unhesitating belief that the unquestioned majorities of both great political parties in this country regard the delay in the working out of a League of Nations as a national and world-wide tragedy.

I can certify the men of all political parties, without any reference to partisan politics, that the same moral and religious forces of this country, because of the inexorable moral issues involved, cannot be silent and will not be silent until there is put forth a League of Nations that will strive with all its might to put an end to the diabolism and measureless horrors of war. . . .

This noble doctrine and heritage of religious liberty calls to us imperiously to be the right kind of Christians. Let us never forget that a democracy, whether civil or religious, has not only its perils, but has also its unescapable obligations. A democracy calls for intelligence. The sure foundations of states must be laid, not in ignorance, but in knowledge. It is of first importance that those who rule shall be properly trained. In a democracy, a government of the people, for the people, and by the people, the people are the rulers, and the people, all the people, are to be informed and trained.

My fellow Christians, we must hark back to our Christian schools, and see to it that these schools are put on worthy and enduring foundations. A democracy needs more than intelligence; it needs Christ. He is the light of the world, nor is there any other sufficient light for the world. He is the one solution of the world's complex questions, the one adequate helper for its dire needs, the one only sufficient Saviour for our sinning race. Our schools are afresh to take note of this supreme fact, and they are to be fundamentally and aggressively Christian. Wrong education brought on the recent World War. Such education will always lead to disaster. . . .

The time has come when, as never before, our beloved denomination should worthily go out to its world task as a teaching denomination. That means that there should be a crusade throughout all our borders for the vitalizing and strengthening of our Christian schools. The only complete education, in the nature of the case, is Christian education, because man is a tripartite being. By the very genius of our government, education by the state cannot be complete. Wisdom has fled from us if we fail to magnify, and magnify now, our Christian schools. These schools go to the foundation of all the life of the people. They are indispensable to the highest efficiency of the churches. Their inspirational influences are of untold value to the schools conducted by the state, to which schools also we must ever give our best support. It matters very much, do you not agree, who shall be the leaders, and what the standards in the affairs of civil government and in the realm of business life? One recalls the pithy saying of Napoleon to Marshal Ney: "An army of deer led by a lion is better than an army of lions led by a deer." Our Christian schools are to train not only our religious leaders but hosts of our leaders in the civil and business realms as well.

The one transcending, inspiring influence in civilization is the Christian religion. By all means, let the teachers and trustees and student bodies of all our Christian schools remember this important fact, that civilization without Christianity is doomed. Let there be no pagan ideals in our Christian schools, and no hesitation or apology for the insistence that the one hope for society, for civilization, is in the Christian religion. If ever the drumbeat of duty sounded clearly, it is calling to us now to strengthen and magnify our Christian schools.

Preceding and accompanying the task of building our Christian schools, we must keep faithfully and practically in mind the primary task of evangelism, the work of winning souls from sin unto salvation, from Satan unto God. This work takes precedence of all other work in the Christian program. Salvation for sinners is through Jesus Christ alone, nor is there any other name or way under heaven whereby they may be saved. Our churches, our schools, our religious papers, our hospitals, every organization and agency of the churches should be kept aflame with the passion of New Testament evangelism. Our cities and towns and villages and country places are to echo continually with the sermons and songs of the gospel evangel. The people, high and low, rich and poor, the foreigners, all the people are to be faithfully told of Jesus and his great salvation, and entreated to come unto him to be saved by him and to become his fellow workers. The only sufficient solvent for all the questions in America, individual, social, economic, industrial, financial, political, educational, moral, and religious, is to be found in the Saviourhood and Lordship of Jesus Christ. . . .

While thus caring for the homeland, we are at the same time to see to it that our program is co-extensive with Christ's program for the whole world. The whole world is our field, nor may we, with impunity, dare to be indifferent to any section, however remote, not a whit less than that, and with our plane sweeping the whole earth, we are to go forth with believing faith and obedient service, seeking to bring all humanity, both near and far, to the faith and service of him who came to be the propitiation for our sins, and not for ours only, but also for the sins of the whole world.

His commission covers the whole world and reaches to every human being. Souls in China, and India, and Japan, and Europe, and Africa, and the islands of the sea, are as precious to him as souls in the United States. By the love we bear our Saviour, by the love we bear our fellows, by the greatness and preciousness of the trust committed to us, we are bound to take all the world upon our hearts and to consecrate our utmost strength to bring all humanity under the sway of Christ's redeeming love. Let us go to such task, saying with the immortal Wesley, "The world is my parish," and with him may we also be able to say, "And best of all, God is with us."

Let us look again to the strange passion and power of the early Christians. They paid the price for spiritual power. Mark well this record: "And they overcame him by the blood of the Lamb, and by the word of their testimony; and they loved not their lives unto the death." O my fellow Christians, if we are to be in the true succession of the mighty days and deeds of the early Christian era, or of those mighty days and deeds of our Baptist fathers in later days, then selfish ease must be utterly renounced for Christ and his cause, and our every gift and grace and power must be utterly dominated by the dynamic of his cross. Standing here in the shadow of our country's capitol, compassed about as we are with so great a cloud of witnesses, let us today renew our pledge to God and to one another, that we will give our best to church and state, to God and to humanity, by his grace and power, until we fall on the last sleep. . . .

8

Until the Next Jubilee

World population will have doubled to exceed six billion people when Baptists of North America celebrate their *next* Jubilee. The population of countries involved in the Third Jubilee Celebration will have climbed from 210,000,000 in 1964 to more than 350,000,000 in 2014, if present population trends continue.

The *World Christian Handbook* for 1962 reports 722,000 places of worship in the world for Protestant and Anglican communions in 1964, representing a Christian community of 264,000,000. The *Handbook* reports 97,000,000 members of Orthodox and Eastern churches, and 494,000,000 members, including children, of Roman Catholic churches. It reports a world population of 13,000,000 Jews, 366,000,000 Moslems, 186,000,000 Buddhists, 316,000,000 Hindus, 300,000,000 Confucianists, 34,000,000 Shintoists, 30,000,000 Taoists, and other smaller groups.

In all of this exploding world population with its divergent religious claims, how will the supreme voice of God in Christ be heard in 2014? What will be the challenge of Baptists to make his witness meaningful among the masses of men?

In an address delivered to the Third Assembly of the World Council of Churches in New Delhi, December 1, 1961, Dr. Donald Coggan, archbishop of York, reported that the Christian proportion of the world population had dropped from 33 per cent in 1940 to 31 in 1960. If this rate of decline continues, he predicted that Christians would comprise only 20 per cent by 2000. These figures would be even more discouraging if projected on to 2014, the next Jubilee for Baptists. We can join with Dr. Coggan when he concluded in saying, "I need not remind an assembly such as this that Almighty God is not subject to the statisticians. There is a Holy Spirit who 'bloweth where he listeth' and who has a way of breaking into history unexpectedly when we do need him most."

It is difficult to forecast the future as far as organic relations are concerned among Baptists in the next fifty years or between Baptists and other groups. To take a dogmatic position on matters of organizational structure for the future is to tempt the judgment of God. But one can make affirmations regarding the person of Christ and the validity of his word, and the leading of his Spirit, which may serve as criteria for judgments in the future.

The strength of the Baptist witness or of the Christian witness in a non-Christian world does not lie in a huge, monolithic structure, but rather in clear objectives and Christlike motivations.

One of the most important elements in organization is the establishment of objectives. One of the problems in our denomination, in our churches, and in our personal lives is that we do not have clearly defined goals. Organizations are meaningless without relevant objectives.

Helmut Thielicke, dean of the faculty of theology in the University of Hamburg, pointed this up in the spiritual realm recently when he said:

The one thing above all that we are saying is that history will surely arrive at its goal. We receive a message that tells there is another who determines this goal, because in His time He will be there, because He will appear on the horizon of the world. One is coming to us from the other side and . . . the world's history will end at his feet. . . . He has told us that at the close the Victor alone will be left on the battlefield, and that on the horizon of our little lives and also on the horizon itself there stands One at whose feet all the zig-zag, circuitous roads of existence will end. Even my little life, lived in this Advent, certainly, is an adventure.

Dr. Harry Emerson Fosdick once said that "the difference between a sermon and a lecture lies in the fact that while a lecture is chiefly concerned with a subject to be elucidated, a sermon is chiefly concerned with an object to be achieved." The difference between our holding a point of view on the gospel and the gospel holding us is related to this matter of objective.

Basically, our objective is the gospel. The good news of God is: "I have come down from heaven, not to do my own will, but the will of him who sent me. It is his will that I should not lose even one of all that he has given me, but raise them all up on the last day. For it is my Father's will that everyone who looks upon the Son and puts his faith in him shall possess eternal life; and I will raise him up on the last day" (John 6:38–40, *The New English Bible*).

Paul recognized this truth clearly when in his letter to the Philippians he wrote: "Let your bearing towards one another rise out of your life in Christ Jesus. For the divine nature was his from the first; yet he did not think to snatch at equality with God, but made himself nothing, assuming the nature of a slave. Bearing the human likeness, revealed in human shape, he humbled himself, and in obedience accepted even death—death on a cross. Therefore, God raised him to the heights and bestowed on him the name above all names, that at the name of Jesus every knee should bow—in heaven, on earth, and in the depths—and every tongue confess, 'Jesus Christ is Lord,' to the glory of God the Father" (2:5–11, *The New English Bible*).

The objectives of the church are not always the same as the stated objectives of the denomination. It might also be disturbing to know that the actual objectives of a church might not always be relevant to the personal needs and concerns of the individual member and, more important, might not always be relevant to the hungry, frightened, sinful man who never darkens the doors of God's house. This is equally true as far as denominational objectives are concerned.

If the members of the 77,000 Baptist churches in North America related to the groups participating in the Jubilee celebration were to appoint committees to make articulate and precise their objectives for the year 2014, there would be a broad spectrum of agreement. Worship, with its full theological meaning, would certainly be at the center. Man's response to God in Christ is at the heart of every Christian experience. Proclamation and witness, the corporate and personal expression of the good news, finds a central place in the experience of all Christian churches. Unfortunately, the personal witness in daily life, in a burning desire to confront other men as persons with a relevant gospel, does not match enough the formal proclamation from the pulpit, statements of faith, and resolutions.

Education is a part of the ongoing objective in practically all 77,000 Baptist churches in the Jubilee. Quantitative goals can be easily set for 2014 in terms of enrolment, subject matter to be covered, and physical equipment to be utilized. It is even more important to determine objectives in the qualitative. Where can techniques be found to replace hatred with love, prejudice with understanding, pride with humility, apathy with compassion?

All Baptist churches consider as an objective, whether stated in formal language or not, some form of ministry. Dr. W. O. Carver, long time professor of missions at the Southern Baptist Theological Seminary, used to say that a church finds its highest expression in the "reality of the fellowship." Dr. Elton Trueblood has described a church as "a fellowship of the concerned." This concern of ministry finds its corporate expression in hospitals, homes for children, aged, and so forth. A church will find its greatest power only when it becomes a loving community.

All of these broad objectives add up to an effective evangelism and a sense of missionary concern which extends even unto the ends of the earth. In these objectives and in the theological convictions which underlie them, there is broad agreement among all Baptist groups representing the 77,000 churches. To be certain there are theological differences, as there will always be within the Baptist concept of the priesthood of the believer under the lordship of Christ; but the range of differences is no greater, for the most part, between the various Baptist groups than it is within the organization of any one group.

The major differences between the Baptist groups in North America are to be found in methodology, sociology, and historical continuity.

In a day when most Protestant and evangelical groups are involved in some form or other of ecumenical pilgrimage, and when even the Roman Catholic Church is seeking to recast its image to present a more positive face to the non-Catholic world, the pressures will be growing during the next fifty years for possible mergers among Baptist groups. As stated previously, this writer does not believe that the strength or weakness of the Christian movement is to be found in the success or failure of a monolithic structure. We believe that the denominational structure is a creature and a servant of the churches rather than the churches finding their life and vitality as creatures of the denominational structure. However, one of the temptations of any bureaucracy is to defend its structure and organization for structure's sake. We must not succumb to this temptation.

The lines of corporate relationship between the various Baptist groups in North America might well remain fixed for the next fifty years, but we must never close our ears to the leading of God's Holy Spirit. Regardless of structural relationship, all will agree as Christians we need to build bridges of understanding to strengthen the witness of a declining Christian percentage of total population in a non-Christian world.

Problems of common concern face Baptists as well as all Christian groups: (1) the growing problem of urbanization with its fortresses of secularism; (2) the problems of racial and ethnic tensions and misunderstanding; (3) the problems of religious groups seeking special favors from the state and special powers in the administration of the state; (4) the ever-present problem of a nuclear holocaust which would wipe out vast centers of population all over the world. These will challenge the creative mind and the daring faith of every Christian during the next fifty years.

Several professors in the California Institute of Technology recently published a book with the title *The Next One Hundred Years.* In this book they seek to forecast something of the population, the raw materials, the energy, the food production, the agricultural resources, and so forth, but these scientists conclude with this consensus:

We have seen that, in principle, man can, if he wills it, create a world where people can lead lives of abundance and creativity within the framework of a free society. It is apparent that there will be many difficulties; there will be many dangers. But it seems reasonably clear what man must do in order that the path may be negotiated. It remains to be seen whether he will recognize these problems in time and proceed to create a still higher level of integration, or whether he will permit his civilization at its present stage of development to disintegrate, perhaps never to reappear. The future of industrial society revolves around the question of whether man can learn to live with man.

Against this background, we might well raise the question asked at the beginning: What are our objectives? How are they related to Christian objectives? How can we be certain that the principles to be followed are Christian? How can we be certain that our objectives lead to the total involvement of the laymen in a daily witness in all areas of life? How can we minimize structure and organization and yet provide clear channels for effective witness? The answers to these questions might well be the answers to many of our problems when we celebrate the next jubilee in 2014.